INGRID ESPELID HOVIG

THE BEST OF
NORWEGIAN
TRADITIONAL
CUISINE

Translation by
Mary Lee Nielsen

GYLDENDAL NORSK FORLAG · OSLO

Typesetting by: Alfabeta as, Halden
Printed in Denmark
Aarhuus Stiftsbogtrykkerie, Århus 1992
Photographs by: Bengt Wilson
Design by: Randi Hoen
Manuscript read by: Jane Finn

ISBN 82-05-20577-9

CONTENTS

FOREWORD

In former times dinner usually consisted of two courses; a main course and either a soup or a dessert. The soup was meant to be so filling that the housewife could economize on the meat or fish, which were expensive.

It is great fun to leaf through old cookbooks and read of the many inventive ways in which the Norwegian housewife prepared fish. Fish so fresh that it flopped under the knife was usually poached to bring out its full flavor and the delicate texture of its flesh.

When a housewife shopped for fish she usually bought enough for two or three meals. Perhaps the fish would be fried on the second day, and then, on the third, the leftovers would be served in one way or another.

Fresh fish was varied with salted, dried and smoked fish, methods of preserving that also gave the flesh a distinctive taste and consistency.

All leftovers, whether meat or fish, were carefully saved and made into new, tasty dishes. Food was a «loan from God». To throw food out was almost as bad as the commission of a deadly sin.

«The Sunday Roast» was a concept in many homes before the war. The roast was often large enough to ensure leftovers for one or even two dinners later in the week.

Roast beef was the favorite for more festive occasions, such as weddings, anniversaries and the like.

The pig was slaughtered at Christmas. For that reason pork is usually associated with winter and the celebration of Yuletide. Roast pork or ham is still traditional Christmas fare in many Norwegian homes today.

Lamb, on the other hand, belongs to fall. On many farms a leg of lamb was far too valuable to eat fresh. The meat was salted and cured, to be put aside and eaten the following summer. Only the wealthy could afford to serve roast lamb.

Fresh meat was formerly often marinated to preserve it for shorter periods of time. Marinating had the added advantage of tenderizing the meat and of enhancing its taste.

Casserole meals in which many ingredients are cooked together in a single dish are by no means a new invention. Stews and soups have long traditions both in Norway and abroad.

«Beta» soup, «burn-snout» and «sodd» are different names for very similar dishes that were often to be found on the menu in this country – inexpensive and satisfying food that still tastes good today. With a ham bone or some beef brisket the housewife could produce flavorful stocks and juicy chunks of meat for very little money. Winter vegetables and potatoes together with barley were added to give body to the dish. The end product was something between a soup and a stew.

Followed by a filling dessert, the main dish could be simple, perhaps just a light soup or leftovers. The dessert might be a sweet soup, a fruit compote, a pudding with fruit sauce or one of many milk-based desserts.

After-dinner cake and coffee is an old Norwegian custom. When father came home from work in the evening, dinner was ready and waiting. After dinner mother washed the dishes and father had his nap. Then it was coffee time. The whole family gathered around the living room table for cakes and coffee – juice for the children.

In former times when life was hard and many Norwegians were poor, cookies and cakes were symbolic of wealth and easy living. The richer the cakes, the more important the occasion and the «finer» the home. Butter and eggs, cream, almonds and candied fruits were an integral part of holidays, birthdays and anniversaries. «Come for coffee and cakes,» is still a current invitation for most Norwegians.

For important celebrations such as weddings and anniversaries, the «bake table» is traditional all over Norway. A bake table may be simple, with just a few cakes, or it may be an elaborate display of innumerable tempting delicacies.

Guests often bring an offering for the bake table, and it goes without saying that the cake that is donated must be a credit to the giver.

In this book you will find many of the familiar, favorite cakes that are often served on special occasions.

For generations both children and adults have counted the days to Christmas from early in December. Some dream of the gifts they hope to receive, others long for quiet, peaceful days spent with family and good friends, but almost all look forward to the smell and taste of the delicious Christmas food that is made just once a year. When the aroma of baking Christmas cakes spreads through the house we know for sure that Christmas is on its way.

Spices were expensive and could not be used daily. But at Christmastime one treated oneself to the very best, as far as one's purse allowed. The smell of clove and cinnamon, cardamom and anise, ginger and pepper, almonds, raisins and candied peel have symbolic ties to the myrrh and incense of the Bible and to the mysteries of the East.

«Flatbread», «lefser», «lapper» and «lumper» are all pancake-like mixtures that are fried on a large, flat skillet, in a frying pan or on special irons. In earlier times they were usually made from barley meal, barley being the one grain that it was possible to grow on Norwegian farms in sufficient quantities to provide the family with its own flour. In our day we are more apt to use a mixture of barley and wheat flours or wheat alone in these recipes.

Porridge is the oldest warm dish in Norwegian food culture. On many farms in the old days porridge was served twice or even three times daily; warm porridge for one meal and cold porridge with warm milk for the next.

Boiled porridge made from water and barley meal, «vassgraut», was most commonly eaten. For variety, the porridge could be made from whole wheat, rye or oat flour, or from whole oats.

But on Saturday evening it was customary to make the porridge with milk, thus marking the difference between the working week and the weekend.

On festive occasions sour cream porridge was often served, a custom that has survived to this day.

FISH
The Norwegian way

GRAVLAX
Gravlaks

All fish that is to be sugar and salt cured, should be frozen for at least 24 hours before or after it has been cured.

The best raw material for gravlax is the middle section of a 6–8 lb. salmon. However, it is entirely possible to use a smaller fish. Cut away the tail piece. It can be dry and is better used for other dishes.

Sea trout may also be used in this recipe.

For every 2 lbs. boned salmon fillet

2 tbsp. salt	1 tsp. coarsely ground
1 1/4 tbsp. sugar	white pepper
	1 large bunch of dill

Clean, wash and fillet the salmon. Cut away the fins and the small bones. Remove bones that stick vertically out of the meat with tweezers or a small pair of pliers. Do not skin the fillets.

Wipe the fillets with paper towels. Mix salt, sugar and pepper and rub the flesh side of the fillets with the mixture.

Place one fillet with the skin side down on an enamel platter or in an oblong dish of stainless steel, glass or plastic.

Rinse the dill well and shake off the water. Chop leaves and stalk coarsely and strew over the fillet. Place the other fillet on top with skin side up, head to tail, the thick neck section against the thinner tail end. Strew a little dill on top.

Cover with aluminum foil. Place a heavy board on top of the salmon. Store the salmon in a cool place, between 45°–50°F. (8–10°C) for 2–3 days. Turn the salmon twice a day and baste with the brine that forms.

Place the salmon in the refrigerator when it is done. Gravlax should be served freshly cured while the flesh is pliant and has a mild flavor.

Serving
Scrape off the dill. Slice the fillets horizontally at a slight angle in paper thin slices. Lay the slices neatly overlapping on a platter and garnish with small, crisp lettuce leaves and fresh dill.

Serve with creamed potatoes and mustard sauce. As an appetizer, gravlax may be served with toasted white bread and butter.

Mustard sauce for gravlax
Gravlakssaus

4 servings

3 tbsp. mustard	3 tbsp. finely chopped
2 tbsp. sugar	dill
1 tbsp. 7 % vinegar	(salt, pepper)
1/4–1/2 cup vegetable oil	

Mix mustard, sugar and vinegar in a small bowl. Add oil a little at a time, beating well between each addition. Add the finely chopped dill. Season to taste with a little salt and pepper.

POACHED COD
Kokt torsk

Poached cod has long traditions in Norway both as everyday food and as party fare. Nothing tastes better than slices of flopping fresh, newly poached cod, even if it is eaten with the simplest accessories and in the humblest surroundings.

4 servings

approximately 4 lbs. cod with head and tail or *2 ¹/₂–3 lbs. cod slices*	**Poaching** *Allow* ¹/₄ *cup salt* 1 *tsp. vinegar for each quart of water*

If your cod has not been gutted, gut it as soon as possible. The quality of the fish deteriorates quickly if the entrails are left in.

Rinse the fish. Cut off the head and one slice just below the pectoral fin. Cut 1 inch thick slices, a little thicker near the tail. Whether you remove the fins or leave them on is a matter of preference.

Wash the fish slices under cold running water. Remove the swimming bladder and the blood along the back bone. A fish brush is a help for this task. Soak slices of very freshly caught cod in cold water for ¹/₂–1 hour.

Place the fish on a platter in the refrigerator if it is not to be cooked at once.

Use a fish poacher or a wide-bottomed kettle. Put in plenty of water. Bring it to a boil, add salt and vinegar and boil again.

Place the cod head and the slice with the pectoral fin in the water first or cook the head separately. Add the other slices.

Let the fish *poach* just below the boiling point until the flesh can be loosened from the backbone with a fork, 3–5 minutes. Cod must be carefully watched. The slices should not cook to pieces.

Place the fish slices on a platter being careful to keep them whole.

Serve poached cod with lemon wedges, and with parsley butter, melted butter or Sandefjord butter (see page 10).

POACHED WHOLE SALMON OR SEA TROUT
Helkokt laks eller ørret

Large fish are best poached in a fish kettle with a rack in the bottom. A large, round kettle or a roasting pan may also be used. The cooked fish will then be temptingly curved on the serving platter. If you don't have a rack to place in the bottom of a round kettle, the fish may be lain on a large piece of aluminum foil with which you can lift the fish from the poaching liquid.

4 servings	For cooking
2 ¹/₂–3 lbs. salmon or sea trout	water 1–2 tbsp. salt for each quart of water
	Poaching time 15–25 minutes

If the fish is to be cooked with its head, remove the gills. Gut and wash the fish well.

Allow enough water to cover the fish. Add salt to the water.

Heat the water to lukewarm and put the fish in the kettle. Bring water to a boil uncovered, over medium heat. Skim well. Poach fish covered over very low heat until done.

The fish is done when the dorsal fin is easily pulled out or when the flesh at the neck loosens from the bone. Test with two forks.

Whole poached fish may be served warm or cold.

If the fish is to be eaten cold it should be cooled in the poaching liquid. Place the kettle in cold water and change the water often, so that the fish is cooled quickly. Refrigerate the fish until it is to be served.

Place the fish carefully on a platter. Remove the skin but leave the fins on.

Warm salmon should be served with melted butter and fresh, boiled vegetables. Cucumber salad (page 11) is also good with poached fish.

Cold salmon is good with sour cream. Add a little horseradish, if you like. Serve with a green salad or cucumber salad (page 11).

SANDEFJORD BUTTER
Sandefjordsmør

In the course of the years the recipe for Sandefjord butter has been experimented with and changed so that many different versions exist today. The original recipe consisted of a little fish stock or water boiled together with lots of chopped parsley. Butter or margarine was beaten in.

Some cooks substitute cream, others white wine for the fish stock. Much more butter is used now than in former times.

4 servings	
¹/₂ cup fish stock or white wine or table cream	4 tbsp. finely chopped parsley ¹/₂ lb. unsalted butter (salt) 1–2 tbsp. lemon juice

Let the butter stand on the kitchen counter until it reaches room temperature. It is best to use unsalted butter when so much butter is called for. Otherwise the sauce may easily become too salty. Season with salt if necessary.

Boil the fish stock, wine or cream with the parsley for 3–4 minutes. Take the pan off the burner. Beat in small dots of butter. The sauce should be smooth and rich.

Do not let the sauce boil after the butter is added. Keep it warm in a double boiler, if necessary.

Season with lemon juice and a little salt if desired.

OLD FASHIONED CUCUMBER SALAD
Gammeldags agurksalat

Some people peel the cucumbers before making salad, others leave the peel on. Some use sugar in the dressing, others prefer it without. Let everyone trust to his or her own taste.

The cucumber is 96 % water. So that the salad would not be soggy and to give the cucumber slices a richer flavor, it used to be customary to sprinkle a little salt on the sliced cucumbers, letting them drain for about 15 minutes and then pressing the liquid out before the dressing was added.

Here is how to prepare cucumber salad in the old way.

4 servings

1 large cucumber
1/2 tsp. salt
(1/2 tsp. sugar)
1 1/2 tbsp. vegetable oil
3/4 tbsp. vinegar
a pinch of white pepper
chopped parsley

Peel the cucumber. Slice it very thin, preferably with a cucumber knife or a cheese plane. Place the cucumber in a bowl. Sprinkle with salt and mix lightly with two forks. Lay a plate on top of the cucumber as a weight. Let the cucumber stand for 15–20 minutes. Press the plate down on the cucumber, squeezing out as much of the liquid as possible.

Mix oil, vinegar and pepper. Pour over the cucumber and mix with two forks.

Serve the salad in a small glass bowl. Sprinkle with chopped parsley.

POACHED SALMON SLICES
Laks kokt i skiver

Poached salmon, warm or cold, was once considered the most luxurious food one could serve one's guests.

May weddings, Whitsun dinners and other spring festivities often featured salmon.

Boiled potatoes, cucumber or green salad, and melted drawn butter were the proper accompaniments to poached salmon.
The fish was accompanied by a sauce of sour cream or lightly whipped fresh cream flavored with a little vinegar, sugar and, if one liked, grated horseradish.

Salmon slices are cooked in the same way whether they are to be eaten warm or cold. In the latter case, add a few whole peppercorns and a small bay leaf to the poaching water for a richer, spicier flavor. Salmon should be cooled in the poaching liquid.

4 servings	Poaching
2–2 1/4 lbs. salmon slices	allow 2 tbsp. salt for each quart of water

Scrape the scales carefully from the skin. Take care not to cut into the flesh. If you are cutting slices from a whole salmon it is easier to scrape it before you slice it. Rinse the fish slices. Remove the blood that clings to the back bone.

Bring the water to a boil, add salt and boil again.

Place the salmon slices in the water and poach them for 12–15 minutes until the flesh is easily loosened from the bone with a fork. Do not overcook or the salmon will be dry.

If the salmon slices are very large, you may place the fish in an empty kettle, arranging the slices neatly. Then baste boiling salted water carefully over the fish until it is well covered.

Bring to the boiling point and let the fish poach until it is done.

Or steam the salmon slices on a rack in a fish kettle.

Garnish the serving platter with green herbs and lemon slices

FRIED MACKEREL WITH SOUR CREAM
Stekt makrell med rømme

Spring and summer mackerel is best suited for frying. In late summer and fall, after the mackerel have spawned, they eat greedily and grow fat. The flesh is then much too rich to fry in butter and simmer in sour cream.

Fall mackerel is best suited for smoking, curing and boiling.

4 servings	
approx. 2 1/2 lbs. small, equal-sized mackerel	3 tbsp. flour 2 tsp. salt
coarsely chopped parsley	2 tbsp. butter or margarine
a little salt	1/2–1 cup sour cream

Clean the mackerel in the round, through the gills without splitting the fish open. Cut off the head and tail. Wash the mackerel well and dry it inside and out with kitchen towels.

Sprinkle the inside of the fish with a little salt, and fill the cavity with plenty of coarsely chopped parsley. If you like you may make a couple of diagonal slits in the thickest part of the flesh so the fish will cook more evenly.

Mix flour and salt on a piece of waxed paper and dredge the fish in the mixture. Fry the mackerel in butter or margarine until nicely browned on both sides. Pour the sour cream over the fish, cover and let the mackerel simmer over low heat until it is done. Baste the sauce over the fish now and then as it cooks.

Check for doneness at the backbone by the neck. The flesh should pull away from the bone when tested with a fork.

Place the mackerel on a platter and pour the sauce over. Sprinkle with chopped parsley, dill or chives.

Serve with boiled potatoes and stewed spinach, or with cucumber salad, green salad or tomato salad.

Poached salmon slices
Laks kokt i skiver

LYE FISH
Lutefisk

For many Norwegians lye fish is synonymous with Christmas, and is always served at Christmas dinner.

Accompaniments to lye fish vary from family to family, traditions passing from parent to child.

Lye fish may either be cooked in a kettle on top of the stove or in the oven.

4 servings
4 lbs. lye fish

Cooking in water
Use a kettle of stainless steel or enamelware. Lye discolors aluminum.

Cut the fish into rather large pieces.

Put a plenty of water in a kettle and bring it to a boil. Add ¼ cup salt per quart of water. Bring to a boil again and put the fish in. Bring just to a boil. Place the kettle over low heat and let the fish stand just below the boiling point for 5–10 minutes. Watch the fish carefully. If it overcooks it may fall apart in the water.

Cooking in the oven
Place the fish pieces with the skin side down in an oven proof casserole or a roasting pan. Sprinkle with 1 tbsp. salt for every 2 lbs. of fish. Cover the pan with aluminum foil. Cook on lowest rack for 30–35 minutes at 375°–425 °F. (200–225 °C).

Serve lye fish right from the cooking pot on heated plates, accompanied by boiled potatoes and melted butter. Fried bacon bits or mustard sauce and flatbread are often served with lye fish. Place the mustard jar and the pepper grinder on the table. Potato «lefse» sometimes accompany lye fish.

POACHED SMOKED HADDOCK
Kokt røkt kolje

Smoked haddock is a favorite with many fish lovers. The fish should not be too small or the flesh will be dry.

4 servings

approx. 2 lbs. smoked haddock	melted butter
water	1 hard-boiled egg

Remove the fins but not the skin and cut the fish into 1 ¼ inch slices.

Place the fish in cold, unsalted water. Bring it just to a boil. Skim and poach the fish over low heat for 8–10 minutes or until the flesh loosens from the bone. Test with a fork.

Serve poached smoked haddock with boiled carrots and potatoes. Pour melted butter with a chopped hard-boiled egg over the fish.

POACHED HALIBUT
Kokt kveite eller hellefisk

Poached halibut may be cooled in the poaching water and served cold with sour cream or mayonnaise, accompanied by a cucumber salad.

4 servings

4 thick slices of halibut,
   approx. 2 lbs.
2 quarts of water
⅛–½ cup salt
2 tsp. vinegar

Rinse the halibut slices quickly in cold water. Let them drain on paper towels.

Bring the water to a boil. Add salt and vinegar and bring to a boil again. Put in the halibut slices and let them poach over low heat for 10–15 minutes. The fish is done when the backbone barely loosens from the flesh. Fish becomes dry if it stays in the poaching water.

Serve halibut right from the pot with boiled potatoes, lemon wedges and parsley butter, Sandefjord butter (see page 11) or hollandaise.

PLUCK FISH
Plukkfisk

Whenever there was poached fish for dinner in the old days enough was almost always cooked so that leftovers could be used the following day. Pluck fish is a fish stew and gets its name from the fact that the leftover fish is plucked into small pieces, and pluck fish appeared regularly on the menu.

Any kind of leftover fish may be used for pluck fish. It is easiest to remove the skin and bones while the fish is warm. If you have cold leftover fish with the bones and skin still on, pour boiling water over it and let it stand a few minutes before cleaning.

Old recipes often recommend putting an extra dot of butter in pluck fish. In our days we try to reduce the fat content in our food, so if you like you may omit the butter or margarine and make the sauce with a flour and water thickening.

4 servings

1 ¼ lbs. cooked, cleaned fish	5 tbsp. flour
	approx. 3 cups milk
1 ¼ lbs. boiled potatoes	salt
¼ cup margarine	pepper
(1 large onion)	(finely chopped chives)

«Pluck» the fish into small bits. Cut the potatoes into small cubes. Chop the onion fine, if you like onion in your pluck fish. Melt the margarine in a pan and fry the onion lightly until translucent. Stir in the flour and add the milk a little at a time, stirring constantly until the sauce is thick enough. Let it boil between each addition.

Let the sauce simmer for 5–10 minutes. Stir now and then so it doesn't stick to the bottom of the pan.

Add the fish and potatoes and let them cook a few minutes until they are heated through. Stir very carefully so the fish is kept as whole as possible.

Season to taste with salt and pepper.

Finely chopped chives may be mixed into the pluck fish or sprinkled over before serving.

Serve crisp flat bread on the side.

PRINCE FISH
Prinsefisk

Legend says that in the last century a Swedish prince visited Bergen. He asked that poached cod be served at the great dinner the city planned to give in honor of his visit. In despair at the impossibility of serving poached cod to such a large gathering, the cook composed a new recipe – «prince fish». The dish was such a success that it has kept its reputation in Bergen to this day and is still considered the finest food you can serve your guests.

The original recipe has disappeared, but in other old recipes both egg yolks and sherry are added to the sauce, and the dish is garnished with lobster and asparagus tips. Champignon and truffles are also mentioned.

In newer recipes shrimp takes the place of lobster, and neatly cut vegetables are often substituted for asparagus. Add lots of finely chopped parsley to the sauce.

6 servings

approx. 2 lbs. cod fillets	1–1 1/2 cups fish stock
1 quart water	(water + fish
1 tbsp. salt	bouillon cube)
	1 1/2 cups table cream
1/2 lb. cleaned shrimp	salt
1 can of asparagus tips	white pepper
	2–3 tbsp. lemon juice
Sauce	or sherry
2 tbsp. butter or	a pinch of sugar
margarine	
3 tbsp. flour	pastry triangles

Rinse the fillets and remove skin and all bones. Keep the fish in as large pieces as possible.

Put fish in boiling, lightly salted water. Preferably use a fish kettle with a rack or a wide bottomed kettle. Poach the fish until the flesh has changed color all the way through. Watch it carefully. It must not overcook and become dry.

The fish may also be cooked in the oven. Place the fillets in a greased baking dish. Pour boiling, lightly salted water over the fish until it is covered. Cover with aluminum foil or waxed paper and place on the middle rack in the oven.

Bake at 375 °F (200 °C) for 10–15 minutes. The fish flesh should change color throughout but still be shiny and juicy.

Heat the asparagus carefully in its juice.

Make a white sauce while the fish is cooking. Melt butter or margarine. Stir in the flour and gradually beat in hot fish stock. Stir the sauce smooth between each addition. Then add cream until the sauce has the right consistency. Let it boil after each addition. After all the cream has been added, simmer for 8–10 minutes. Season to taste with salt, pepper and lemon juice or dry sherry. Add a pinch of sugar for a smoother flavor.

Take the fish out of the poaching water as soon as it is done. Use a skimmer so the water runs off, or let the fish drain on the fish rack before serving on a warm platter. If any fish stock accumulates on the platter, pour it carefully off or mop it up with paper towels. Extra stock will thin the sauce.

Pour the hot sauce over the fish and garnish with well drained asparagus, shrimp and pastry triangles. Serve with boiled potatoes sprinkled with chopped parsley.

FISH BALLS FROM FINE FISH DOUGH
Fiskeboller

Fish balls are made from the same dough that is used in fish loaf. See page 22.

Fishballs are also delicious served with shrimp sauce.

Bring to a boil fish stock or lightly salted water (2 tsp. salt to each quart of water).

Smooth the surface of the fish dough. Shape small balls with a spoon dipped in cold water or larger ones about the size of a golfball, with a wet spoon and the palm of your hand. Place the balls in the boiling liquid.

The liquid should be kept just at the boiling point when the fish balls are added. Poach them over low heat for 5–10 minutes or until done. If fish balls are cooked too hard, they will lose their shape and will not be as flavorful.

Turn the balls once. Place the cooked fish balls to drain on a platter.

FRIED TROUT
Stekt ørret

Delicious, small mountain or brook trout are best fried whole, so one can delight in the fish's lovely color and shape.

Fry it crisp in butter or simmer it in sour cream, as you prefer.

4 servings

4 small fresh water trout, 10–13 oz, each	¼ tsp. pepper
	2 tbsp. butter or margarine
3 tbsp. flour	(½–1 cup thick sour
2 tsp. salt	cream)

Clean and wash the trout. Remove the gills and dry the fish well with paper towels.

Mix flour, salt and pepper in a plastic bag.

Brown a little butter or margarine in a frying pan. Dredge the fish in the flour and place them in the frying pan.

Fry golden brown over medium heat. The fish should be cooked through without getting too brown. If the dorsal fin loosens from the bone at the neck, the fish is cooked.

If the trout is to be cooked in sour cream, add it when the fish is thoroughly browned and simmer in the cream until done.

Serve with cucumber salad (page 11) and boiled potatoes.

FISH LOAF IN SHRIMP SAUCE
Fiskepudding i rekesaus

Ground haddock makes the best fish loaf. Haddock binds exceedingly well and ensures a light and pliant fish dough. For best results, follow these simple rules: stand in a cool place while working; be sure that the fish is fresh and cold; be sure the milk and cream are very fresh and ice cold; stir the ground fish until stiff before adding the liquid; and finally, add the liquid slowly, a little at a time, and beat it stiff between each addition.

6 servings

2 lbs. fish fillets,	*2 tbsp. potato flour or*
haddock or pollack.	*cornstarch*
All bones removed.	*¹/₄ tsp. mace*
2 tsp. salt	*approx. 2 ¹/₂ cups milk*

Rinse the fillets under running cold water. Dry them with paper towels. Cut the fillets in pieces and grind them once in a meat grinder. Add salt and potato flour or cornstarch and grind the fish 2–4 more times. It is important that the fish dough is as firm and stiff as possible. The oftener it is ground the finer the texture of the resulting dough.

Beat the fish dough with an electric beater and add the milk, 1–2 tbsp. at a time, beating the dough stiff after each addition. When half of the milk has been added you may add 3 tbsp. at a time.

If you wish, you may substitute cream for ¹/₄–¹/₂ cup of the milk. Always add the cream last.

Successful fish dough should be smooth and fine textured at all times. It is important to stand in a cool place while you work.

Add the mace.

Poach a sample fish ball to test the flavor and consistency.

Grease a 6 cup mold. Let the fat harden. Pour in the fish dough. Fish loaf does not rise, so the mold may be filled to the rim. Smooth the surface carefully. Tap the mold against the table top to pack the fish dough well in the mold, avoiding air holes in the cooked loaf.

Place the mold in a roasting pan, and put the pan in the oven. Fill the roasting pan with boiling water. Cook the loaf about 1 hour at 250 °F. (120 °C). Press the top of the loaf with the back of a spoon. When it feels firm it is done.

Let the fish loaf stand a few minutes in the mold before turning it out.

Serve shrimp sauce with fish loaf.

Shrimp sauce

1 ¹/₂ tbsp. butter or	*1 ¹/₂ cups milk and*
margarine	*1 cup fish stock*
2 ¹/₂ tbsp. flour	*¹/₂ tsp. salt*
approx. 2 ¹/₂ cups milk	*3 ¹/₂ oz. cleaned, cooked*
or	*shrimp, fresh, frozen*
	or canned

Melt butter or margarine in a heavy bottomed saucepan. Add the flour and stir well. Add the liquid gradually, stirring constantly. Simmer the sauce for about 5 minutes after the last of the liquid is added.

Add the shrimp. If canned shrimp are used, the stock in the can may be substituted for part of the milk in the sauce.

If the shrimp are pre-cooked, the sauce should not boil after they are added or they will be tough.

FISH CAKES OF FINE FISH DOUGH
Fiskekaker

Use the same dough as for fish loaf and make your own fish cakes.

Brown a little butter or margarine in a frying pan. Shape the cakes with a wet spoon and the palm of your hand and place them in the pan. Or make large cakes with a spoon. Smooth the surface of the cakes in the frying pan.

Fry fish cakes over medium heat. If the pan is too hot the cakes will swell and deflate.

Fish loaf in shrimp sauce
Fiskepudding i rekesaus

BACALAO

First rate clipfish – salted and dried cod – should be white and fine, with meaty pieces that swell to twice their size during soaking. Clipfish is now usually sold ready packaged, cut into serving-sized pieces.

Clipfish should be soaked for 12–24 hours before it is prepared. Put the fish in cold water and change the water a couple of times during the soaking period. Take the thinnest pieces out after about 12 hours and refrigerate them until the rest of the fish is sufficiently soaked. If the fish soaks too long it will lose its inimitable flavor.

6 servings

2 lbs. clipfish	4 garlic cloves
12–15 raw potatoes	1 small can of tomato
6 tomatoes	paste (2 1/2 oz.)
2 large onions	2 tbsp. paprika
1 large red bell pepper	3/4 cup olive oil
l large green bell pepper	1 1/4 cup water

Soak the fish for 12–24 hours. Skin, and remove all bones.

Peel the potatoes and cut in slices about 1/4" thick. Peel the onions. Coarsely chop half of one onion and slice the rest. Slice the tomatoes. Remove seeds and membrane from the peppers and slice them.

Place a wide, heavy-bottomed kettle over low heat and pour in the oil. Fry the onions translucent in the oil. Place tomato slices, pepper slices, fish, potato slices and onion slices in alternating layers in the kettle. The top layer should be potatoes.

Sprinkle fish layers with paprika and spread tomato paste between the layers.

Pour in the water

Simmer over low heat. Shake the kettle now and then so the bacalao does not stick to the bottom.

The bacalao is done when the potatoes on top are barely soft. Serve right from the kettle, accompanied by fresh rolls or French bread.

POLLACK CAKES
Seikaker

Homemade pollack cakes, right out of the frying pan, are a treat. If you buy fish fillets and have a grinder attachment on your electric mixer, they are easy to make or use a food processor. Pollack cakes make a fine Sunday evening supper and, eaten in rolls with slices of tomato, onion and a pickle, they are a delicious substitute for hamburgers. Fishburgers will be sure to make a hit.

4 servings

1 lb. pollack fillets, with all bones removed	1 1/2 tbsp. potato flour or cornstarch
1 tsp. salt	1/4 tsp. pepper
	approx. 3/4 cups milk
	margarine for frying

Grind the fish once. Beat the dough stiff with the salt, pepper and potato flour (cornstarch).

Add the milk gradually.

Brown a little of the margarine in a frying pan. Make large cakes with a wet spoon and your hand and place them in the pan. Press the cakes a bit flat with a spoon.

Brown the cakes over medium heat. Reduce the heat and fry them slowly over low heat for about 10 minutes until they are cooked through. Turn them a couple of times.

Serve pollack cakes with plenty of fried onions. Or make a brown sauce and heat the cakes in the sauce. Or serve them with creamed vegetables.

Boiled potatoes go well with pollack cakes.

Bacalao

24

FISH ASPIC WITH REMOULADE
Fiskekabaret med remuladesaus

Aspics have been a decorative part of the Norwegian buffet table for generations. If an aspic is to be really delicious there should be lots of good ingredients in it. The gelatin must not dominate but merely hold all the ingredients together.

Fish aspic may be made with various vegetables, shellfish, hard-boiled eggs and cooked fish, white or dark, according to one's individual taste.

Serve with remoulade and crusty French bread.

6 servings

1 ½ lbs. fish fillets	*2 tsp. white wine*
boiling water	*vinegar or white 5 %*
2 tbsp. salt for each	*vinegar*
quart of water	*1 can asparagus*
	spears, 12 ½ oz.
2 tbsp. gelatin	*7 oz. cleaned small*
4 cups boiling, well	*shrimp*
flavored fish stock	*1 package of frozen peas*
	(petit pois)
	1 tomato

Skin the fish and remove any bones. Cut it into large pieces. Boil the water, add salt. Add the fish and poach until it has changed color throughout. Cool the fish in the cooking water. Drain on absorbent paper.

Dissolve the gelatin in boiling stock according to instructions on the package. Add the rest of the stock and season with a little vinegar.

Pour ½ cup of the gelatin in a 1 ½ quart oblong mold. Refrigerate the mold until the gelatin has set.

Strain the liquid from the asparagus. Place asparagus on absorbent paper to drain. Cut off the tops in equal lengths. Cut the rest into smaller pieces.

Cut the tomato in narrow wedges. Scrape away the soft insides.

Remove the mold from the refrigerator when it is set. Arrange the asparagus tops, shrimp, tomatoes and peas in a neat pattern on the set gelatin. Remember that the underside will be on top when the aspic is unmolded. Decorate the sides of the mold with shrimp.

Put the fish, the remaining shrimp, peas and asparagus pieces in the mold. Reserve some of the vegetables if there is too much to fill the mold.

Pour cold, still liquid gelatin carefully into the mold. Refrigerate until it sets.

There will probably be leftover aspic. Pour it onto a platter, refrigerate and let set. Before serving, chop it coarsely and use it to decorate the platter beside the aspic. An aspic should be made a day ahead so that it has time to set thoroughly.

Before serving, dip the mold into hot water a moment so that the gelatin loosens along the sides of the mold. Place a platter over the mold and invert to unmold.

If you leave the mold in the hot water too long the gelatin will melt and the surface of the aspic will not be smooth.

Remoulade

4 servings

¾ cup mayonnaise	*3 tbsp. chopped parsley*
½ cup low fat sour	*3 tbsp. chopped capers*
cream	*a little lemon juice or*
3 tbsp. chopped gherkin	*pickle brine*
pickles	

Mix all ingredients and season to taste with lemon juice or pickle brine. The capers may be omitted, in which case use 6 tbsp. chopped gherkin pickles. This is a mild, delicious sauce.

Fish aspic with remoulade
Fiskekabaret med remuladesaus

MEAT
For everyday meals and
special occasions

ROAST LAMB
Lammestek

Roast lamb is a true Norwegian's favorite meal. Nowadays it is usually served rare or medium rare, but many people still prefer the old way – well done.

In former times small bunches of parsley were slipped into incisions in the roast and it was seasoned with pepper, but Central European ways are gradually winning favor in Norway, and many now prefer to insert slivers of garlic in the meat and season it with herbs.

Vegetables for roast lamb are boiled green beans, peas, broccoli, Brussels sprouts, braised pearl onions, fried mushrooms, baked tomatoes or a fresh green salad.

6–8 servings	Gravy
1 roast lamb, 4–5 lbs.	3 cups pan drippings
1 $^1/_2$ tsp. salt	and bouillon
1 tbsp. butter or	2 $^1/_2$ tbsp. flour
margarine	$^1/_2$ cup cold bouillon or
$^1/_2$ tsp. pepper	water
1 tsp. rosemary	(caramel coloring)
1 tsp. thyme	salt
1 tsp. basil	
(2 garlic cloves or	
1 bunch of parsley)	
3 cups boiling water	

If the lamb is frozen it should be thawed slowly in the refrigerator for a couple of days. Cut away the inspection seal carefully so the outside membrane is not pierced.

Wipe the roast with a damp cloth or dampened paper towels.

If you like the flavor of garlic, stick a clove of garlic well into the meat along the bone, or insert slivers of garlic into slits cut in the meat with a sharp pointed knife. Or the roast may be flavored with parsley in the same way. Pluck the leaves from the stem and push them into each incision. Rub the roast with salt. Mix butter or margarine with the herbs and spread over the roast.

Put the meat into a roasting pan with bone side down. Stick a meat thermometer into the thickest end of the roast, making sure it doesn't touch the bone.

Preheat the oven to 250–300 °F. (125–150 °C).

When meat is roasted at a low temperature it is extra juicy and shrinks less.

Put the roasting pan on the bottom rack in the oven. After 30 minutes pour 1 $^1/_2$ cup of water in the pan. Add the rest of the water after an hour.

When the meat thermometer reaches 160 °F. (70 °C) the meat will be pink inside.

At 170 °F. (76 °C) it is well done.

Allow 2–2 $^1/_2$ hours roasting time, but watch the thermometer carefully so the meat is not over done.

Take the roast out of the oven when it is done. Remove the roast to a platter and cover with aluminum foil to keep it warm.

Let it rest for 15–20 minutes before carving. The juices will spread throughout the meat and less will run out when it is carved.

Measure the pan drippings. Deglaze the roasting pan with a little water to get the drippings that stick to the bottom. Add more water or bouillon so there is enough liquid for the gravy.

Skim the fat off the drippings.

Make a thickening of flour and cold bouillon or water. Bring the liquid to a boil and stir in the flour and water thickening. Simmer the gravy for 5–10 minutes. Strain the gravy, if desired. Season to taste with salt and pepper, and add a few drops of coloring if it is very pale.

Lamb gravy should not be too dark.

LAMB STEW
Lammefrikassé

Don't forget lamb stew! Juicy, tender lamb, cooked just right, with autumn's fresh, crisp vegetables is a pleasure for the eye and the palate.

Root vegetables such as carrots, celeriac, rutabaga and parsley root are traditional in lamb stew, but you may also
use cauliflower florets, peas, green beans and leek.

All parts of the lamb are tender in stew. Therefore it is a good way to use the front end of a lamb. Buy meat from the neck, shoulder, breast or shank. Avoid fatty meat.

3–4 servings

2 lbs. lamb	Gravy
boiling water	2 $\frac{1}{2}$ cups meat or
1 $\frac{1}{2}$ tsp. salt per quart	vegetable stock
of water	4 tbsp. flour
3 carrots	1 cup cold stock or
$\frac{1}{2}$ celeriac or 2 stalks	water
celery	(salt, white pepper)
or	finely chopped parsley
2 parsley roots or	
2 parsnips	

The meat should be cut into bite-sized pieces. Rinse the meat in lukewarm water, one piece at a time. Place on absorbent paper to drain.

Pour the water into a kettle and bring it to a boil. Add salt and then the meat. The water should cover the meat completely. Pour off excess water.

Bring to a boil uncovered. Skim. Simmer covered until the meat loosens from the bone, about 1 $\frac{1}{2}$ hours.

Clean and wash the vegetables. Cut the celeriac into thick slices and cut the carrots in two, lengthwise, if desired. Boil the vegetables in a separate saucepan in lightly salted water until they are barely done.

Strain the meat stock when the meat is tender. Skim off fat.

Measure the stock for gravy. Bring to a boil.

Pour cold water or stock into a small jar with a tight cover and add the flour. Screw cover on well and shake until the mixture is smooth, without any lumps, or make a thickening in the usual way.

Stir the mixture into the boiling stock. Let the gravy simmer for about 10 minutes. Add more stock if the gravy is too thick. Stew gravy is best when it is a bit thick. Season to taste with more salt and white pepper.

Place the meat on a warm platter. Cut the vegetables into cubes with a serrated vegetable knife, if you have one, and spread them over the meat.

Pour a little of the warm gravy over the meat and vegetables and sprinkle with finely chopped parsley.

Serve with boiled potatoes and pour the rest of the gravy in a gravy boat.

PORK PATTIES
Medisterkaker

Pork Patties are shaped and fried as meat patties.

4 servings

1 lb. ground pork,	or
including 15–20 %	1 $\frac{1}{2}$ tbsp. all purpose
pork fat	flour
1 $\frac{1}{2}$ tsp. salt	$\frac{1}{4}$ tsp. pepper
1 $\frac{1}{4}$ tbsp. potato flour	$\frac{1}{4}$ tsp. ginger
	1 $\frac{1}{4}$ cups milk

Mix salt, potato flour or flour and seasonings with the ground meats. Add the cold milk a little at a time. Shape patties and fry as meat patties (page 39).

Lamb stew
Lammefrikassé

ROAST OF BEEF, OR VENISON MARINATED IN BEER
Ølmarinert roast

Beer marinades come in endless variations. The greatest difference is in the type of beer used. Connoisseurs say that unadulterated beer, straight from the bottle, is the best marinade. They recommend using a dark beer for dark meat and a pale beer for lighter meat.

4–5 servings	For roasting
approx. 2 lbs. beef, or venison – shoulder cut	*2 tbsp. butter or margarine*
Marinade	**For boiling**
2 ½ cups beer	*1 cup marinade*
¼ cup vinegar, 5 %	*1–1 ½ cups water*
2 red onions, finely chopped	**Sauce**
1 bay leaf	*2 cups pan juices*
5 white peppercorns	*2 tbsp. flour*
	½–1 cup cream
	salt, pepper

Remove fat and membranes. Place the meat in a plastic bag. Mix all the ingredients for the marinade and pour it into the bag. Tie the top. Place the bag on a platter and refrigerate for 3–6 days. Turn the bag from time to time.

Remove the meat from the marinade.

Brown the butter or margarine in a pan. Brown the meat on all sides.

Take the pan off the burner and pour the marinade and boiling water into the pan. The liquid should reach half way up the sides of the meat.

Bring to a boil and let the meat simmer over low heat for about 1 hour. Turn the meat after half an hour.

Remove the meat from the pan and wrap it in aluminum foil to keep it warm.

Strain the cooking juices and measure them for the gravy. Make a paste of flour and cream and beat it into the boiling juices. Simmer the gravy for 5–10 minutes. Add more pan juices, stock or cream if the gravy is too thick. Season to taste. Serve with boiled potatoes.

MEAT'N GRAVY
Sausekjøtt

«Sosekjøtt» as it is called in Bergen and much of Western Norway is often served at Sunday dinner or as the main course at informal gatherings.

In other parts of the country the dish is called «Meat in the Dark».

Meat 'n gravy is a tasty alternative to boiled meat. The dish is easily made, it is filling and relatively inexpensive.

4 servings	
3 lbs. beef – flank, shoulder or chuck	*2 tbsp. butter or margarine*
4 tbsp. flour	*2 onions*
1 tsp. salt	*approx. 3 cups of water*
½ tsp. pepper	

Wipe meat with a damp cloth and dry it. Cut it into serving pieces.

Mix flour, salt and pepper in a plastic bag. Shake the meat in the flour until coated. Brown meat in butter or margarine. Don't put too many pieces in the frying pan at once as that will lower the temperature and make browning difficult.

Place the meat in a saucepan. Deglaze the frying pan with a little of the boiling water after each portion is browned and pour liquid into the pan.

Peel the onion and cut it into thin strips. Sauté lightly in the rest of the fat until translucent. Add to the meat. Add the rest of the water to the level of the top pieces of meat.

Simmer for 1 ½–2 hours or until the meat is tender and the gravy thickened. Shake the pan now and then so the meat doesn't stick to the bottom and burn.

If you wish a thicker gravy you may add a little flour and water thickening. Darken the gravy, if desired, with a little caramel coloring.

Serve with boiled potatoes and creamed peas or creamed cabbage. Lingonberry jam is a tasty accompaniment to Meat'n Gravy, or try cranberry jam.

POUNDED STEAKS
Bankekjøtt

This dish gets its name from the fact that the meat was pounded with a mallet to tenderize it before cooking.

«Bankekjøtt» used to be considered a little fancier than Meat'n Gravy. The meat was boneless and trimmed. Many will certainly remember «bankekjøtt» from their childhood with mixed emotions. The dish can be mild and tasty, but at times it is so highly seasoned with bay leaves that it is hard to swallow.

Beware therefore of using too much bay, and leave it out altogether if you think someone may not like its flavor.

4 servings

1 ½ lbs. boned, trimmed beef from the shoulder	1 onion
	1 small bay leaf
5 tbsp. flour	5 whole black pepper-
1 ½ tsp. salt	corns
¼ tsp. pepper	3–4 cups water or
3 tbsp. butter or margarine	bouillon (cube)

Have the butcher cut the meat into ¼ inch slices. Wipe it with paper towels.

Peel the onion and cut it in strips.

Brown the onion in a little of the fat and put it in a pan.

Mix flour, salt and pepper in a plastic bag. Dredge the meat in the flour mixture and brown it in butter or margarine in a frying pan. Put the meat in the pan with the onion.

Add seasonings and pour over boiling water or stock. The liquid should be level with the top of the meat.

Bring to a boil and let the meat simmer, covered, over low heat for about 1 hour or until it is tender. Turn the pan now and then, so it doesn't stick to the bottom.

Season the gravy to taste. Add a little caramel coloring, if desired.

Serve with boiled potatoes and boiled vegetables such as cauliflower, peas, carrots, beans.

ROLLED ROAST OF BEEF
Roastbiff

Roast beef, boned and rolled, is served cold on the buffet table.

Thinly sliced roast beef is also a favorite for open-faced sandwiches.

4–5 servings

approx. 2 lbs. sirloin strip, rump or round	¼ tsp. pepper
1 ½ tsp. salt	2 tbsp. butter or margarine

Remove any fat or membranes from the meat. Truss it with cotton string so the meat has a cylindrical shape.

Brown the meat well on all sides in a frying pan, in butter or margarine. Don't forget to brown the ends.

Use two wooden spoons to turn the meat so you don't pierce the surface. Place the meat in a small oven proof pot or a roasting pan. Season with salt and pepper and insert a meat thermometer horizontally into the meat from one end.

Roast the beef on the middle rack of the oven at 250 °F. (125 °C) until the thermometer reaches the desired temperature.

At 130 °F. (55 °C) the meat will be rare, at 140 °F. (60 °C) medium rare.

In such a slow oven it will take about one hour for the center of the meat to reach 130 °F. (55 °C).

Let the roast rest for about 20 minutes before carving it. Use a sharp knife and cut very thin slices.

Serve sautéed mushrooms and small onions, green beans, broccoli and young green peas with roast beef prepared in this way.

CABBAGE ROLLS WITH WHITE SAUCE
Kålruletter med hvit saus

The best cabbage rolls are made with the leaves of early cabbage or freshly harvested fall cabbage.

4 servings
*12 medium sized
   cabbage leaves*

Stuffing
*1 lb. meat patty mix
   (page 39) or meat
   loaf mix*

Boiling water
*1 tsp. salt per quart
   water
2–3 carrots*

White sauce
*2 tbsp. butter or
   margarine
2 tbsp. flour
2–2 ½ cups milk
salt*

Choose a medium large head of cabbage.

Boil the water in a large kettle. Put the head of cabbage in the boiling water and cook for 5–10 minutes. Cut the leaves loose at the stem end and remove them carefully.

Place the cabbage leaves in the kettle and cook them a few more minutes. Immerse the leaves quickly in cold water, so they are chilled and retain their light green color.

Turn the leaves out on a cloth or a rack and drain well. Slice off some of the thick stem from the leaves so they are thinner and easier to roll.

Put a big spoonful of stuffing on each leaf. Wrap the cabbage well around the stuffing in a little package and tie with cotton string.

Add a little salt to the boiling cabbage water. Place the cabbage rolls in the water and simmer for 20–30 minutes until the stuffing is cooked through.

Put the rolls on a rack or cloth to drain. Remove the string.

Make a white sauce: melt the butter or margarine in a saucepan. Stir in the flour and add the milk gradually. Stir smooth after each addition. Simmer for 5–10 minutes. Stir now and then. Season to taste with a little salt.

Arrange the cabbage rolls on a platter with boiled, sliced vegetables.

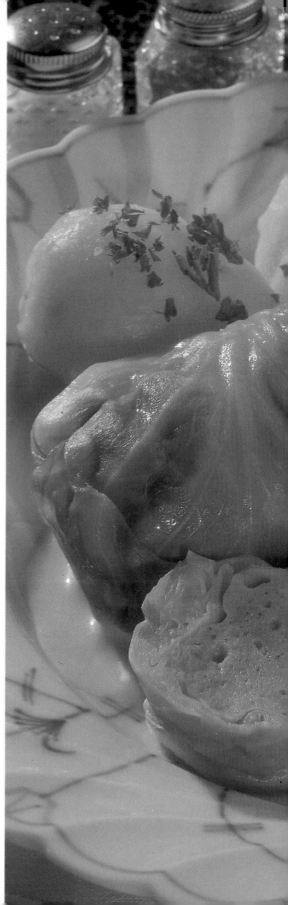

BOILED BEEF AND BROTH WITH ONION SAUCE
Ferskt kjøtt og suppe med løksaus

Boiled beef and broth is a favorite cold weather meal. Use meat from the forepart of the animal, with as little fat as possible so the meat will be juicy. The fat may be cut off before serving.

Tie a leek, some celery leaves and a few stalks of parsley together and cook them in the broth to give both meat and broth extra flavor.

4 servings	Onion sauce
3 lbs. – beef with bone – flank, shoulder, chuck, rib or loin	2 tbsp. butter or margarine
approx. 2 quarts water	1 onion
2 tsp. salt	3 tbsp. flour
2–3 carrots	2 ½ cups meat stock
2 parsley roots or ½ celeriac	(salt)
approx. ¼ head of cabbage	1–2 tsp. vinegar
a «soup bunch», 2–3 leek leaves, 2 celery leaves and 3–4 parsley, stalks tied together	1–2 tsp. sugar

Have your butcher crack the bones without cutting the meat. Rinse the meat. Cut away any inspection seals.

Cut away any big bones. Put the bones and any meat that clings to bone in a kettle with cold, salted water. Bring to a boil uncovered. Skim.

Add the meat. Bring to a boil and skim again. Add the soup bunch and let the meat *simmer* very slowly, covered, until tender, about 2 hours.

Test for doneness by sticking a cake tester or skewer into the meat. If it goes in easily and the meat loosens from the bone it is done.

Clean the vegetables and cut them into small pieces with a knife, preferably a serrated vegetable knife, if you have one. Cut the cabbage in thin wedges. Add the vegetables to the soup for the last 10–15 minutes of cooking. If preferred,

boil the vegetables separately in a little of the broth. If you like, cut some of the vegetables into julienne strips when they are done and serve them in the soup. Remove the tied «soup bunch» and squeeze out the juices. Strain the stock that is to be used for sauce.

Make the sauce as follows:

Peel and finely chop the onion. Sauté it lightly until translucent in butter or margarine in a small saucepan. Stir in flour and add the warm stock a little at a time, stirring after each addition.

Simmer for 5–10 minutes and season to taste with salt, vinegar and sugar. The sauce should have a mild, sweet-sour flavor.

Serve the piping hot broth with some of the vegetables as a first course. Cut the meat into smaller pieces and serve it as a main course with the vegetables, boiled potatoes and onion sauce.

Boiled beef and broth with onion sauce
Fersk kjøtt og suppe med løksaus

BEEF BIRDS
Benløse fugler

This is a traditional dish. In the old days the «birds» were stuffed with beef marrow or fat and seasoned with both clove and ginger. Now, most people prefer to stuff the «birds» with chopped parsley, cheese and prosciutto or anchovies and chopped onions.

4–5 servings

1 lb. hamburger meat	or
¼ lb. ground pork	1 ½ oz. diced
1 ½ tsp. salt	prosciutto
¼ tsp. pepper	1 ½ oz. diced Jarlsberg
1 egg	or other Swiss-type
½ cup finely mashed	cheese
potatoes	or
approx. ¾ cup milk,	8–12 anchovy fillets
cream or water	1 tbsp. chopped onion

Stuffing

butter or margarine for frying

2 tbsp. butter or
   margarine
3–4 tbsp. chopped
   parsley
or
2 ½ oz. marrow or
   pork fat
¼ tsp. pepper
a pinch of ginger
a pinch of clove

Brown sauce

2 tbsp. butter or
   margarine
4 tbsp. flour
approx. 2 cups bouillon
   or water
salt
pepper
(caramel coloring)

Make the sauce first.

Melt the butter or margarine in a small saucepan. Add the flour and stir over medium heat until the mixture is cinnamon brown. Don't let it get browner or it will taste burned.

Take the pan off the burner and add half of the hot bouillon or water. Stir the sauce until smooth. Add the rest of the liquid. Simmer sauce over low heat 5–10 minutes. Season to taste with salt and pepper. Color, if desired, with caramel coloring.

Mix the hamburger meat and ground pork. Add salt and mix well. Add pepper and the lightly beaten egg.

Add the boiled potatoes a little at a time, to the meat mixture. Knead until pliant. Add the liquid.

Dampen a cutting board with cold water. Spread the meat on the board and press or roll meat mixture to a ½" thick rectangle. Cut into 12 equal rectangles. Spread the stuffing of your choice in equal amounts in the middle of each rectangle. Wrap the meat around the stuffing to make smooth rolls, about 4 inches long, and 1 inch in diameter.

If you use marrow or fat as stuffing, mix the seasonings and sprinkle a strip in the middle of each meat oblong before adding the stuffing.

Brown butter or margarine in a frying pan. Brown the «birds» on all sides.

Put the «birds» in the sauce and simmer over low heat for 10–15 minutes until cooked through.

Season sauce to taste.

Serve beef birds in the sauce with boiled potatoes, boiled vegetables and lingonberry or cranberry jam, pickles or other condiments.

UP-COUNTY SOUP or «SODD»
Innherredsodd

«Sodd» is traditional company food in Northern Trøndelag –
the administrative area surrounding the city of Trondheim. Follow all the rules if you want the best results. «Sodd» is no ordinary meat soup.

A lot of work goes into good «sodd», but sodd is worth the work.

In Northern Trøndelag a special type of flat bread called «skjenning» is served with «sodd». The flat bread is brushed on one side with a mixture of milk and sugar as it is fried so that this side is shiny and a bit sweet. This adds an extra flair to the «sodd».

Crisp, thin flat bread may also be served with up-county soup.

8 servings
3 lbs. meat from a loin
    of beef or leg of lamb
approx. 2 quarts water
2 tsp. salt

Meatballs
2 lbs. ground beef/
    hamburger meat
1 tbsp. salt
2 tbsp. potato flour or
    all purpose flour
2 eggs

2 cups milk
approx. 2 ¼ cups
    heavy cream
a pinch of nutmeg

boiling, lightly salted
    water

3–4 carrots

potatoes

Rinse the meat. Place it, in one or two pieces in lightly salted, boiling water. Bring to a boil uncovered and skim well. Simmer over low heat until tender, about 2 hours.

Remove the meat when it is done. Cool meat and stock separately.

Stir the ground meat with the salt to stiffen. Add flour and egg. Add milk, a tablespoon at a time. Stir well between each addition. Add cream, 2 tablespoons at a time. Add nutmeg.

Make small meatballs with a teaspoon dipped in cold water. Simmer the meatballs for about 5 minutes. Turn them once.

Put the balls to drain. The «sodd» may be prepared in advance to this point.

Remove bones, membranes and fat from the meat and cut it in 1 ½ inch dice.

Remove the fat from the cooled meat stock. Pour the stock carefully into a kettle, keeping back the residue in the bottom of the pan. Bring stock to a boil. Skim if necessary. Season with a little ground mace. Heat the meat cubes in a little of the stock.

Heat the meatballs in the rest of the stock. Do not use the water that the meat balls were cooked in.

Boil potatoes and carrots separately. Julienne the carrots – with a serrated vegetable knife, if you have one. Keep them warm in the carrot water. The carrots should not be heated with the meat or the meatballs as the soup would then be too sweet.

Place individual servings of meat, meatballs and carrots in each soup bowl and ladle the broth over.

Serve the boiled potatoes on the side.

SALTED LAMB RIBS
Pinnekjøtt

«Pinnekjøtt» means, literally, twig meat, referring to the rack of twigs in the bottom of the pan. «Pinnekjøtt» is a favored Christmas dish.

4 servings
3 lbs. lamb ribs from
    the breast
a little boiling water

Dried and salted lamb ribs may be purchased in shops that sell Norwegian specialties.

If you want to prepare the ribs yourself, you should buy meat with narrow ribs, a sign that the lamb is young. If there is too little fat the meat will be dry.

Rub the ribs with salt and place them in a tub with a layer of salt in the bottom. Sprinkle salt over the ribs. Refrigerate and let stand in the salt for 36–48 hours. Scrape the salt carefully off the ribs and hang them to dry in a well ventilated, dry and cool place for 2–3 months.

Cut the meat along the ribs and crack the ribs in the middle. A small hack-saw is good for this job. Soak salted lamb ribs overnight in plenty of cold water.

Arrange stripped birch twigs crisscross as a rack in the bottom of a heavy bottomed kettle or use an aluminum rack. Add water so it barely touches the under side of the rack or the top layer of birch twigs. Place the meat on top. Cover tightly and place a heavy weight on the cover. Bring to a boil over high heat and steam the meat over medium high heat for 2–3 hours, depending on the age of the lamb the meat came from. Take care that the kettle doesn't boil dry. Add a little boiling water along the sides of the kettle if necessary, making sure the water does not touch the meat itself.

The meat is done when it loosens from the bone.

Salted lamb ribs must be served piping hot on warm plates. The juices in the bottom of the kettle are used as gravy. Serve with mashed rutabaga and boiled potatoes.

POTATO DUMPLINGS WITH MEAT, SALT PORK and RUTABAGA
Kumler med kjøtt, flesk og kålrot

Norwegian potato dumplings have many names. They are called «kumler», «kompe», «raspeball» or «klubb», depending on what part of the country you come from.

Some cooks put meat or salt pork in the dumplings, others serve the meat on the side. Some serve potato dumplings with a sauce made with brown Norwegian goat cheese (geitost), while others pour melted butter over their dumplings. Recipes and traditions vary from place to place and from home to home.

This recipe was used in my home.

4–6 servings	Potato dumplings
1 ½ lbs. salted and (optional) smoked mutton	1 lb. raw potatoes, peeled
approx. 1 lb. salt pork	approx. ¼ lb. boiled potatoes
3 quarts water	1 tsp. salt
	¾–1 cup barley flour
	2–3 tbsp. flour
	1 small rutabaga
	melted butter
	thyme

Soak the meat and the salt pork overnight. Bring to a boil, uncovered, in fresh cold water. Skim. Simmer meat and salt pork, covered, until tender, about 1–2 hours. Remove from pan and keep warm in a little of the stock.

Grate the raw potatoes on the finest part of a grater or grind them in a food mill with the finest attachment. Mash or grind the boiled potatoes and mix the two. Add salt and flour at once so the potatoes don't darken. If the potatoes have a high water content you should pour off some of the water before the flour is added or you will have to add more flour and then the dumplings will be too firm.

The amount of flour needed depends on the quality of the potatoes. Make a sample dumpling to test this. The mixture should not be so thin that the dumplings spread out into the stock, nor should they be so firm that they are heavy and tough.

Shape the dumplings with a tablespoon dipped in the warm stock and drop them into the simmering stock. The meat stock should simmer at all times while the dumplings are cooking. The kettle should be so large that there is plenty of room for the dumplings or they may stick together. Simmer for about 30 minutes or until they are cooked through. Cut a dumpling in two to test it.

Peel the rutabaga and cut it into bite-sized pieces. Boil tender in a little of the meat stock or in lightly salted water. If there is room in the kettle, the rutabaga may be cooked with the dumplings.

Cut the salt pork in slices and the meat in cubes. Place meat, pork and rutabaga on a platter with the dumplings. Serve, using the melted fat skimmed from the stock or a little melted margarine as a sauce. Some people prefer fried salt pork and pork fat with potato dumplings.

Season the stock to taste with salt and thyme and serve as a soup with the dumplings or alone, the next day.

Potato dumplings with meat, salt pork and rutabaga
Kumler med kjøtt, flesk og kålrot

AUBIN – MEAT STEW WITH MASHED POTATO CRUST

It is fun to stick to the foreign names that were sometimes used to give recipes for leftovers a touch of elegance. Aubin is the French term for meat and highly seasoned gravy.

To make this a company dish and to use up left-over potatoes, the stew is covered with mashed potatoes and browned in the oven.

You can use left-over boiled or roasted meat. With instant mashed potatoes and a package of gravy mix you should have a meal that is both tasty and quickly made.

4 servings

	Mashed potatoes
3 cups leftover meat, diced	2 ¼ lbs. boiled potatoes
2 ½ cups brown gravy, or use canned beef gravy	¼–½ cup milk
	1 tbsp. butter or margarine
(2–3 tbsp. wine or sherry)	1 egg
¼ tsp. pepper	salt
½ tsp. paprika	or 1 package instant
(leftover vegetables)	mashed potatoes

Season the gravy well with pepper, paprika and a little wine, if desired. Add the cooked meat. Add vegetables such as peas, sliced carrots or the like.

Put the stew in an oven proof mold.

Mash the boiled potatoes and add milk, margarine and a lightly beaten egg. Save a little of the egg to brush the potato topping.

Or make instant mashed potatoes according to the instructions on the package. Add a beaten egg.

Cover the stew with the mashed potatoes and smooth the surface. Make a pattern with a fork and press a little of the potato through a pastry tube to decorate, if desired.

Brush the top with beaten egg and place the casserole on the middle rack of the oven. Bake at 350 °F. (175 °C) until golden brown.

The oven should not be so warm that the gravy boils through the potato topping. Serve with a green salad.

CREAMED SALT PORK
Stekt flesk med duppe

A few years ago one of Norway's larger newspapers asked its readers to name the recipe they had liked best as children.

Creamed salt pork won, hands down! The dish is very filling, so use lean salt pork.

4 servings

1 lb. salt pork, not too salty	1 cup low fat sour cream and 1 ½ cups milk
2 tbsp. flour	a dash of pepper
2 cups milk or	
	finely chopped chives

Cut the rind off the pork and cut it in thin slices across the grain of the meat.

Put the salt pork in a frying pan and pour cold water over it. Bring to a boil and pour off the water.

Rinse and dry the frying pan. Put the pork in the dry, warm frying pan and fry it golden brown. Remove the pork. Sprinkle the flour in the fat and stir well. Add milk or sour cream and milk. Low fat sour cream is apt to curdle but has a pleasant, sour flavor.

Simmer the sauce for a few minutes. Season to taste with a little pepper. Add the salt pork and sprinkle with chopped chives before serving.

Serve with boiled potatoes and boiled rutabaga.

Aubin – meat stew with mashed potato crust

SALT PORK PANCAKES
Fleskepannekaker

A childhood dream was to be allowed to eat salt pork pancakes whenever one liked. But pancakes took time to fry and there were always many mouths to feed, so the dream never came true.

These thick, egg-yellow cakes dotted with green, chopped chives should certainly tempt today's youth as well?

If you find it difficult to turn the pancakes on the cover, as described in the recipe, you may fry more and thinner pancakes from the batter and turn them with a pancake turner.

Approx. 3 servings

$\frac{1}{2}$ cup flour	4 eggs
$\frac{1}{4}$ tsp. salt	finely chopped chives
2 cups milk	
	approx. $\frac{1}{2}$ lb. salt pork

Put flour and salt in a dry bowl. Add 1 $\frac{3}{4}$ cups of milk and stir until smooth. Add the rest of the milk. Beat in one egg at a time.

Let the mixture stand and swell for at least 30 minutes. Add the chopped chives.

Slice the pork and cut the slices into 1 inch pieces. If the pork is very salty you can de-salt it as follows: place the salt pork in a non stick frying pan and add cold water. Bring to a full boil. Pour off the water and dry the pork with paper towels.

Wash and dry the frying pan and fry the pork golden brown.

You should be able to make three thick pancakes from this recipe. Leave $\frac{1}{3}$ of the pork in the pan with the fat. Pour $\frac{1}{3}$ of the pancake batter over the pork. Fry the cake over low heat until it is light brown on the under side and nearly firm on top. Turn the pancake carefully with a pancake turner. Fry the cake lightly on the other side.

Place the pancake on a round platter when done. Fry the other two pancakes in the same way and stack all three on top of each other, as they are finished. Cut the whole heap of pancakes in wedges as you would a cake. Serve with lingonberry or cranberry jam or a salad.

YELLOW PEA SOUP
Gul ertesuppe

Few meals from our childhood are recalled with such pleasure as thick, flavorful, yellow pea soup with fresh waffles right from the iron or thin Norwegian pancakes with jam for dessert.

Stock from ham hocks or some other salted meat makes the best pea soup. Bouillon cubes may be used, of course, but they will not give the same tasty result.

Dried peas should be soaked overnight.

Dried peas cook faster if you put a tablespoon of salt in the soaking water.

4–6 servings

2 cups dried yellow peas	cold water
	1 onion
water + 1 tbsp. salt for soaking	($\frac{1}{2}$ tsp. thyme)
	stock from ham or other salted meat
	$\frac{1}{2}$ leek
	pepper

Put the peas to soak in salted water overnight. Pour out the soaking water and rinse the peas.

Add fresh cold water to completely cover the peas. Bring to a boil. Skim well. Add the coarsely chopped onion and the thyme, if desired, and simmer the peas until they are done, 1 $\frac{1}{2}$–2 hours.

Add meat stock until the soup has the right consistency. Finely slice the leek and add it to the soup for the last 10 minutes of the cooking time. Season to taste with pepper and adjust the saltiness with the stock or with more salt.

The meat from the ham hocks or other cooked salted meat can be diced and added to the soup. Or add a cooked pork sausage, cut in dice. Serve with flat bread or slices of fresh whole wheat bread.

Salt pork pancakes
Fleskepannekaker

50

GAME

PTARMIGANS
Ryper

Ptarmigans may be purchased plucked and drawn. The giblets are usually packed in a small bag in the body cavity.

Sometimes, however, one gets unprepared birds into the kitchen. Then you must pluck and draw the ptarmigan before cooking.

8 servings

4 ptarmigans	1 cup sour cream
3–4 tbsp. butter	3–4 juniper berries
2 cups boiling water	a little currant jelly
2 cups boiling milk	a thin slice of brown
1 cup sour cream	goat cheese (geit-
approx. 1 tsp. salt	ost), optional

Wash the plucked and drawn ptarmigans and the giblets under running, cool water. Dry both inside and outside well with paper towels. Dry the giblets.

Truss the birds so that legs and wings are held tightly to the body. Brown the butter in an iron pot. Brown birds well on all sides over moderately high heat, being sure not to burn them. Brown the giblets and neck with the bird for the last few minutes. Sprinkle with salt.

Pour the boiling water and milk in the pot. Cover, but leave a large opening on one side. Simmer with breast up for about 25 minutes. Baste with the cooking liquid at regular intervals. Add sour cream and the crushed juniper berries. Continue simmering for about 15 minutes or until the ptarmigans are tender. Test them by carefully inserting a cake tester.

The cooking time depends on the age of the ptarmigans. Old birds can be tough.

Remove the ptarmigans from the pot. Strain the stock. Rub solids through the sieve and add to the stock.

Puré the liver, heart and gizzard in a food processor or chop them very fine. Beat the giblets into the sauce. If the sauce is too thin it may be thickened with 3–4 tsp. of flour stirred to a smooth paste in a little water or sour cream.

Simmer sauce a few minutes. Season to taste with salt, a little currant jelly or a slice of brown goat cheese, «geitost».

Divide the ptarmigans in two. Arrange them on a platter and ladle a little sauce over each half. Serve the rest of the sauce piping hot on the side.

Brussels sprouts, peas, mushrooms, lingonberry or cranberry jam, rowan or currant jelly all go well with ptarmigan. And, of course, boiled potatoes.

Ptarmigan may be prepared a day ahead. When they are done, lay the half ptarmigans overlapping, like shingles, in an oven proof casserole or in a roasting pan. Pour a little of the sauce over them. When they are cold, cover with aluminum foil. Refrigerate until just before serving. Heat them for about 30 minutes in a 250 °F. (125 °C) oven. Arrange them on a platter or serve them in the casserole.

Heat the sauce and serve as above.

Ptarmigans
Ryper

BRAISED REINDEER
Dyrestek i gryte

Other kinds of venison, such as stag or moose, may be substituted for reindeer in this as well as in the following recipe.

In Norway, reindeer is usually sold as frozen, boned, rolled roasts, packed in elasticized nets.

4 servings

	Sauce
approx. 2 ½ lbs. reindeer – from round, shoulder or loin or approx. 1 ½ lbs. boned, rolled reindeer	3 cups braising liquid
	3 tbsp. flour
	½ cup cold milk for thickening
2 tbsp. butter or margarine	½ cup heavy cream or sour cream
1 tsp. salt	(caramel coloring)
1 ½ cups water	1 thin slice brown goat cheese (geitost), optional
1 ½ cups milk	
½ cup sour cream	salt
8 juniper berries	

Half thaw the frozen roast. Wipe it thoroughly. Sear the meat on all sides in the butter or margarine. Do not use such high heat that the meat burns. Remove the pan from the burner. Add boiling water and milk. Sprinkle with salt and crushed juniper berries. Insert a meat thermometer.

Simmer the meat covered over low heat for about 1 ¼ hours or until the thermometer reads 170 °F. (76 °C). Turn the meat when it is half done. Add the sour cream at that time.

Remove the meat from the pan when it is done. Strain the braising liquid. Press the solid ingredients through the sieve and add to the sauce.

Measure the stock. Add more stock or water so there is enough for the sauce. Make a thickening of cold milk and flour. Beat the thickening into the boiling stock. Add cream or sour cream and a little brown Norwegian goat cheese «geitost». Color with a few drops of caramel coloring, if desired. Simmer the sauce for 10–15 minutes. Season to taste.

ROAST REINDEER
Dyrestek i ovn

Reindeer meat is lean and may be dry. That is why it is best immediately after cooking.

All vegetables go well with reindeer, but those with lots of flavor are best – such as Brussels sprouts, broccoli, small onions and canned or frozen green beans or peas.

Lingonberry or cranberry jam and rowan jelly are excellent accompaniments to all game.

8 servings

Approx. 5 lbs. reindeer – from shoulder, round or loin or approx. 4 lbs. rolled, boned reindeer	Sauce 4 cups pan juices mixed with stock or water 1 cup cold milk 4 1/2–5 tbsp. flour
3 tbsp. butter or margarine	8–10 juniper berries 1 cup sour cream
2 tsp. salt	2 slices brown goat cheese (geitost), optional
2 cups boiling water 2 cups boiling milk	salt (a little currant jelly)

Place the meat on a rack in a roasting pan. Insert the meat thermometer. Spread a little butter on the roast. Cook on the lowest rack in the oven at about 250 °F. (125 °C) until the thermometer reads 170 °F. (76 °C). Pour boiling water and milk into the roasting pan when the meat is half done, after about 1 1/2 hours. Add the crushed juniper berries. Baste at intervals with the pan juices. Deglaze the roasting pan. Strain the juices and make sauce as under braised reindeer (page 54).

Both braised and roasted meat should «rest» for about 20 minutes before carving. Slice thin. Baste a little sauce over the slices on the platter. Serve the rest of the sauce in a gravy boat.

Allow about 1/2–3/4 cup of sauce per person.

If you want to prepare the roast and sauce a day ahead, the meat thermometer should read no more than 163 °F. (73 °C).

Slice the cold roast in relatively thin slices. Store them packed together in aluminum foil in convenient packages. Place the wrapped meat over the burner or in a 240 °F. (120 °C) oven for about 30 minutes before serving. The packages of meat may also be heated in a double boiler.

ØSTERDALEN MOOSE
Elgstek fra Østerdalen

Moose hunting and the preparation of moose has long traditions in the forests of Eastern Norway, along the river Glomma. Almost a third of this country's total moose population is found in the county of Hedmark, and each year several thousand moose are killed in that area.

The meat of the moose is lean. It may be prepared as game or as beef.

5-6 servings

3 lbs. moose – from the round, shoulder or loin	For braising 1 tsp. salt
1–2 whole onions	1/4 tsp. pepper 4 cups water
For browning 2–3 tbsp. butter or margarine	Sauce 2 tbsp. butter or margarine 2 tbsp. flour 3 cups cooking liquid 1 cup sour cream

Wipe the meat well with a damp cloth or paper towels.

Peel the onion.

Brown the butter or margarine in a heavy bottomed pan.

Sear both the onion and the meat well. Take the pot off the burner. Sprinkle the meat with salt and pepper and pour the boiling water into the pot beside the meat.

Simmer the meat, covered, over low heat for about 1 1/2 hours. Turn the meat after half the cooking time.

Brown the butter or margarine and the flour for the sauce cinnamon brown in a saucepan. Measure the cooking liquid and pour half in the butter and flour roux. Then add the rest, half at a time. Stir well between each addition, so the sauce will not be lumpy. Beat in the sour cream and simmer the sauce for 5–10 minutes. Season to taste.

Carve the meat in thin slices and arrange it on a platter. Cut the whole, browned onion in pieces and spread over the meat.

Serve with boiled potatoes, boiled carrots, Brussels sprouts and peas.

WOOD GROUSE
Stekt tiur og røy

Freshly killed birds should hang and ripen for 5–6 days. In cold weather they may hang longer. Leave the entrails in the birds.

The birds must, however, not hang so long that they are damp under the wings or in the body cavity and begin to smell strongly.

Roast only young wood grouse. The breast bone on young birds is pliant and cartilaginous at the base. The skin on the legs should be smooth, it should have a sharp beak and sharp claws.

Wood grouse has dark meat with a gamey flavor. The average weight is about 4 $\frac{1}{2}$ lbs. One bird is enough for 6–8 servings.

The hen or «røy» weighs about 3 lbs. and serves 5–6.

5–8 servings

1 wood grouse (about 4 lbs.) or 1 wood grouse female (about 3 lbs.)	1 $\frac{1}{2}$ tsp. salt 1 $\frac{1}{2}$ cups sour cream
salt pepper 2 $\frac{1}{2}$ oz. bacon or thinly sliced salt pork 2–3 tbsp. butter or margarine approx. 3 $\frac{1}{2}$ cups boiling water approx. 3 $\frac{1}{2}$ cups boiling milk	**Sauce** 3-4 cups pan juices 2-3 tbsp. flour 1 cup cold milk or water salt pepper a little currant jelly (caramel coloring)

Thaw frozen wood grouse in a cool place for about 2 days. Pluck when half thawed. The feathers are then easier to remove.

Cut the bird open and remove the heart, gizzard and liver. Wash the bird and the giblets. Dry both thoroughly with paper towels.

Rub the bird with salt and pepper. Truss the bird so the wings and legs are held tightly against the body. Cover the breast with thin slices of bacon or salt pork. Tie the pork to the body.

Brown butter or margarine in a pot. Brown the bird on all sides. Brown the giblets toward the end. Add the boiling milk and water, mixed. The liquid should reach half way up the side of the bird. Sprinkle with a little salt. Cover and simmer over low heat, with breast up, for 2–3 hours. The pot may also be placed covered or uncovered in an 300 °F. (150 °C) oven.

Baste the bird often during cooking whether it is cooked on the stove or in the oven. Add more liquid if too much evaporates during cooking.

Remove the bird from the pot. Wrap it in aluminum foil to keep warm. Strain the pot liquid, pressing solid ingredients through the sieve before adding to sauce. Skim fat. Measure the liquid and add more stock or bouillon if necessary to make enough sauce. Make a thickening of flour and cold milk (or cream), and beat into the boiling liquid. Simmer for 5–10 minutes. Chop the giblets and add to sauce. Season to taste with salt and pepper and a little currant jelly, if desired.

Cut the breast meat from the bone and slice it. Divide the legs at the joint. The meat from the second joint can be sliced. Arrange the meat on a platter and ladle a little sauce over it. Serve the rest in a gravy boat on the side.

Serve with boiled potatoes or fried potato balls, fried or creamed mushrooms, a green salad or Waldorf salad, or boiled vegetables such as Brussels sprouts and peas. Currant or rowan jelly is a good accompaniment.

Black grouse (orrfugl) is prepared in the same way as wood grouse. The female weighs about 2 lbs. and will serve 3. The male weighs about 3 lbs. and serves 5.

Black grouse should cook about 1 $\frac{1}{2}$ hours.

TRADITIONAL DESSERTS

YOGHURT BAVARIAN
Surmelksfromasj med rød saus

This is a mouth-watering dessert. It is mild and yet tasty, with a piquant flavor of vanilla and a light, airy consistency. Yoghurt Bavarian is served with red sauce.

The Bavarian may be made the day before it is to be eaten.

4–5 servings

2 ¹/₂ cups yoghurt	20 scalded almonds
4 tbsp. sugar	3 tbsp. raisins
1 tsp. vanilla	1 ¹/₂ tbsp. gelatin
1 cup heavy cream	¹/₄ cup water

Finely chop the almonds.

Soften gelatin in the cold water for 10 minutes.

Beat the yoghurt well with the sugar and vanilla. Add almonds and raisins.

Beat the cream stiff and fold it in.

Dissolve the gelatin over boiling water.

Cool the gelatin mixture a little and beat it into the yoghurt in a thin stream.

Stir now and then until it begins to thicken so that the raisins and almonds won't settle on the bottom of the bowl.

Rinse a mold in cold water and pour in the Bavarian.

Tap the mold against a towel on the counter top to break any air bubbles in the mixture. Refrigerate the Bavarian for 4–5 hours to set.

Before serving, dip the mold in hot water for a moment. Place a platter over the mold and invert it. If it is difficult to unmold the Bavarian you may lay a towel wrung out in hot water over the mold or dip it again in hot water.

Red Sauce
4–5 servings

³/₄ cup strongly flavored currant, raspberry or other juice	1 ³/₄ cups water – taste to be sure the juice is not too weak
	(sugar)
	1 level tbsp. potato flour, cornstarch or arrowroot

Regulate flavor of the juice by using more or less water and juice.

Pour juice and water in a saucepan. Add sugar to taste. Stir in potato flour or cornstarch.

Place pan on stove top and stir while bringing to a boil.

Serve sauce cold with the Bavarian.

Yoghurt Bavarian
Surmelksfromasj med rød saus

MOLDED VANILLA CREAM
Fløterand med friske bær

Vanilla cream with fresh berries is often served as dessert at dinner parties in Norway, or on the cake and dessert table. The mild, creamy flavor is well suited to all kinds of berries and fruit.

6–8 servings

	Filling
3 cups heavy cream	1 quart fresh berries
3 tbsp. sugar	sugar
1 tsp. vanilla	or
1 tbsp. gelatin	the same amount of sugared frozen berries

Soak the gelatin in a little cold water for about 10 minutes.

Whip the cream barely stiff with sugar and add the vanilla.

Dissolve the gelatin in a metal cup over hot water. Cool for a few minutes and beat it into the cream in a thin stream.

Rinse a ring mold with cold water and pour the cream in. Tap the bottom of the mold against the counter top to settle the cream and break any air bubbles. Smooth the surface.

Refrigerate the mold for 3–4 hours until the cream is set.

Dip the mold in hot water for a moment. Place a platter over the mold and invert it to unmold.

Fill the center of the ring with fresh, sugared berries or with partly thawed frozen berries. Garnish with a few of the best berries and sprigs of mint.

COLD BOWL
Kaldskål

On a warm summer day, there is nothing that tastes as refreshingly delicious as a big helping of Cold Bowl. The dessert should be refrigerated for 20–30 minutes before serving.

4–5 servings

4 cups yoghurt	whole oats toasted
juice of ½ lemon	in a dry frying pan
3 tbsp. sugar	zwieback or rusks
½ tsp. vanilla	fresh strawberries
1 cup heavy cream	
coarsely chopped	
almonds or	

Beat the sour milk well. Add lemon juice, sugar and vanilla. Beat the cream stiff and add it.

Sugar to taste.

Sprinkle with chopped almonds or toasted whole oats.

Serve cold bowl in soup dishes with crushed rusks or zwieback on top and fresh strawberries on the side.

CARAMEL PUDDING
Karamellpudding

For many, many years, caramel pudding has been the classic party dessert above all others.

A successful pudding should be smooth textured, showing a fine, velvety cross-section when cut. There should be no small bubbles in the pudding. If the result is not up to expectations, it may be that the eggs were whipped too much or that the oven was too warm.

Recipes for caramel pudding may vary. Some are made with heavy cream, some with a mixture of milk and cream and some with just milk. A pudding made with milk is light and tasty.

4 servings

¾ cup sugar for the caramel	4 tbsp. sugar
	1 tsp. vanilla
4 eggs	3 cups milk

Heat a 1 quart loaf pan on the stove top. Heat a frying pan on another burner. Add the sugar. Spread it out over the whole bottom of the pan and do not stir until it starts to melt. Stir constantly as the sugar browns, and crush any lumps. Brown to the color of caramel. Drip a little of the hot caramel on a white plate to check the color. The caramel must not be so brown that it tastes burned.

Pour the caramel into the heated bread pan. Use thick pot holders and tip the bread pan so that the caramel coats the bottom of the pan and runs part way up the sides. Hold the pan away from you so that you don't risk getting the caramel on your hands. Hot caramel can cause serious burns. Cool the form.

Break the eggs in a bowl and beat them with a fork or egg beater until the whites and yolks are thoroughly mixed, but do not mix more. Too much beating can cause bubbles in the pudding. Add sugar and vanilla to the cold milk. Add eggs. Strain the mixture before pouring into the loaf pan to avoid white threads of egg white in the pudding. Pre-heat oven to 300 °F. (150 °C).

Place the pan in a roasting pan on the bottom rack of the oven. Pour boiling water in the roasting pan and cook the pudding for 50–60 minutes.

The water in the roasting pan must not boil while the pudding bakes or there will be bubbles in the pudding. If the water in the roasting pan starts to boil, add a little cold water.

Insert the point of a sharp knife into the middle of the pudding to see if it is done. Remove the pudding from the oven, but leave the pan with the hot water in to cool. It is risky to move a pan full of hot water. Cool the pudding. It should be refrigerated overnight before it is unmolded.

Carefully loosen the pudding along the sides with a knife. Place a platter on top and invert the mold. The caramel that sticks to the pan may be melted with a little boiling water. Cool and pour over the pudding on the platter.

If you like, serve caramel pudding with a bowl of whipped cream on the side.

CHOCOLATE PUDDING WITH VANILLA SAUCE
Sjokoladepudding med vaniljesaus

Chocolate pudding with vanilla sauce ranks second after caramel pudding in the list of favorite desserts. Here is the original recipe from the days when all food had to be prepared from scratch.

4 servings

4 tbsp. cocoa	3 cups milk
6 tbsp. sugar	1 ¹/₂ tsp. vanilla
5 level tbsp. cornstarch	

Mix cocoa, sugar, cornstarch and the cold milk in a saucepan. If the cocoa is lumpy, sift it before use. Add the milk, a little at a time to begin with, and stir after each addition. Place the saucepan over medium heat and bring to a boil, stirring. Let the pudding boil a couple of minutes. Stir constantly.

Season to taste with vanilla.

If the pudding is to be unmolded, pour it into a mold that is first rinsed in cold water.

Cover the pudding while it cools, so a skin doesn't form on the top.

Chocolate pudding that is not to be unmolded need not be so stiff. Use only 4 tbsp. cornstarch.

Vanilla sauce

2 cups milk	2 egg yolks
3 ¹/₂ tbsp. sugar	¹/₂ cup milk
¹/₂ tsp. vanilla	1 tbsp. cornstarch

Bring the milk to a boil with the sugar. Add vanilla.

Beat the egg yolks, cornstarch and ¹/₂ cup of cold milk in a bowl. Beat in the boiling milk. Pour back in the saucepan and stir over medium heat until the sauce thickens. The sauce must not boil or it will separate.

Pour the sauce in a bowl or pitcher to cool. Sprinkle a little sugar on top so a skin does not form.

Beat the sauce before serving.

MOONLIGHT PUDDING
Måneskinnspudding

Can you think of a more romantic name for a dessert? If you let your imagination go you can almost see the moonlight on the snow as the golden sauce flows down the sides of the white pudding.

4 servings

zest and juice of	1 ¹/₂ cups heavy cream
1 lemon	3 egg whites
3 tbsp. sugar	
1 tbsp. gelatin	3 egg yolks
¹/₈ cup water	3 tbsp. sugar

Stir the gelatin into the water. Soak 10 minutes and dissolve over hot water.

Wash and dry the lemon. Grate the zest. Squeeze the juice and strain it. Mix the zest and juice with the sugar and the dissolved gelatin.

Beat the cream and egg whites stiff in separate bowls. Beat the lemon mixture into the cream and fold in the beaten egg whites. Rinse a mold in cold water and pour the pudding in it. Refrigerate to set.

When the pudding is set, dip the mold in hot water and unmold. Beat the egg yolks and sugar until the sugar is dissolved and pour over the dessert just before serving.

TROLL CREAM OR «A THOUSAND AND ONE NIGHTS»
Trollkrem eller «Tusen og en natt»

You may use either fresh or frozen berries in this light and fluffy dessert.

4–5 servings

1 quart lingonberries	³/₄-1 cup sugar
or if they are not	1 egg white
available try cran-	¹/₄ tsp. vanilla
berries.	

Mix berries, sugar and egg white. Stir with a wooden spoon or with the electric mixer until the sugar is dissolved and the mixture fluffs up. A little vanilla gives a fuller flavor.

NORWEGIAN OMELET SURPRISE WITH HOME MADE ICE CREAM OR BAKED ALASKA
Is surprise med hjemmelaget iskrem

Before the days of freezers, before inexpensive ice cream was available, and before home ice cream machines could be bought, ice cream was only served on very special occasions.

This dessert is a real «surprise». The cold, hard ice cream wrapped in a hot meringue is considered one of the «great» desserts. With modern methods it is not difficult to make. You can use a ready-made sponge cake and any brand name ice cream. But should you wish to try ice cream made in the old way, here is a recipe for 6 servings.

Sponge cake

4 large eggs	*1 cup flour*
³/₄ cup sugar	*1 tsp. baking powder*

Whip eggs and sugar stiff, until the sugar is completely dissolved 8–10 minutes.

Mix flour and baking powder and fold into the egg mixture. Pour into a well-greased 9 inch cake pan with a removable rim. Bake the cake on the middle rack of the oven at 375 °F. (200 °C) for about 30 minutes. Turn out onto a rack. Cool.

Vanilla ice cream

1 vanilla bean or	*³/₈ cup powdered*
1 tsp. vanilla	*sugar*
¹/₂ cup water	*3 egg yolks*
	1 ¹/₂ cups heavy cream

Cut lengthwise along the vanilla bean to open it. Put it in a saucepan (not aluminum) with the water. Add 2 tbsp. of the powdered sugar and simmer 10–15 minutes. Remove the vanilla bean and add the rest of the powdered sugar. Rinse the vanilla bean and let it dry. It may be used again.

Take the pan off the heat and beat in the egg yolks, one at a time. Heat the mixture, stirring constantly, until it is thick and creamy. Do not boil.

Remove the pan from the heat again and continue stirring until slightly cooled. Cool completely. Season to taste with vanilla if you have not used a vanilla bean.

Whip cream stiff and add the custard. Pour into a loaf pan that holds about 6 cups. Place in freezer for 3–5 hours, until completely frozen. The ice cream may be made well in advance.

Berries for filling

1 ¹/₂ cups fresh or	**Meringue**
frozen raspberries	*3 egg whites*
a little sugar or	*¹/₂ cup sugar*
³/₄ cup raspberry	
jam	

Beat egg whites stiff. Add sugar a little at a time and whip until the meringue is stiff and keeps its shape.

Garnish
approx. ¹/₄ cup almond
flakes
(fresh berries)

Preheat oven to 475 °F. (250 °C).

Slice the sponge cake in half horizontally. Cut one of the halves so that it is the same size as the mold the ice cream was frozen in. If necessary, piece with the bits cut from the sides.

Place the sponge cake on an oven proof plate.

Spread cake with jam or sugared berries.

Take the ice cream out of the freezer. Dip the mold a moment in hot water and unmold on the jam covered cake.

Put the plate with ice cream and cake in the freezer while you whip the meringue.

Cover the top and sides of the ice cream completely with the meringue. Sprinkle with almond flakes.

Bake on the middle rack of the oven for 3–5 minutes until the meringue is golden brown. Watch carefully so it doesn't burn!

Serve as soon as it comes from the oven, first decorating with a few berries, if desired.

ARCTIC DESSERT
Russedessert

They knew how to make a lot out of a little in the old days. With nothing but juice, water, sugar and semolina you can make a big bowl of this delicious dessert. Just try!

4–5 servings

2 cups of concentrated juice, currant or other red fruit juice	(sugar)
	¹/₂ cup semolina or farina
2 cups of water	

If the juice is not strong enough add less water and more juice. Taste to be sure.

Bring juice and water to a boil and add sugar to taste. Beat in the semolina or farina and simmer for about 15 minutes. Stir now and then so it doesn't stick to the pan.

Pour the porridge in the bowl for your electric mixer and beat until it is completely cold, pale, light and airy.

You may also beat the pudding with a rotary beater. Put the bowl in cold water to cool faster.

Serve arctic dessert with vanilla sauce, cream or milk.

SEMOLINA PUDDING
Semulepudding

An everyday dessert that was often used in the old days and that both adults and children would surely like just as well today.

The pudding is not as stiff if you add a beaten egg to the warm mixture as soon as it is cooked. The semolina must not boil after the egg is added.

Semolina pudding may be set in a mold and unmolded before serving. Rinse the mold in cold water before pouring in the pudding. Refrigerate until set.

Loosen the sides of the pudding with a small knife and let in a little air around the edges. Turn the pudding out on a platter.

4 servings

1 quart milk	2 ¹/₂ tbsp. sugar
¹/₂ cup semolina or farina	3–4 drops of almond flavoring

Bring the milk to a boil and beat in the semolina. Simmer for 20 minutes. Cover the pan but stir from time to time so the pudding doesn't stick to the bottom of the pan and burn.

Add sugar and almond flavoring to taste. Be careful not to use too much almond. Count the drops in a teaspoon instead of pouring right into the pan.

Pour the pudding into a bowl. Cover so a skin doesn't form on the surface. Cool the pudding and serve it with red sauce (page 58).

RED PUDDING
Rødgrøt

Even though red pudding is nothing but thickened fruit juice and water children have always considered it an extra special dessert. Red pudding feels velvety smooth on the tongue.

4 servings

4 cups of concentrated fruit juice and water.	(sugar)
	4 tbsp. potato flour or cornstarch

Pour the juice and water into a saucepan. Taste. It should be stronger than juice for drinking. Add sugar if necessary. Stir the potato flour or cornstarch into some of the cold juice and add it to the pan. Bring to a boil, stirring constantly.

Cool the dessert in the pan. Pour it into a glass bowl. Sprinkle with a little sugar to avoid a skin on top.

Serve red pudding cold with cream or milk.

Arctic dessert
Russedessert

VEILED FARM GIRLS
Tilslørte bondepiker

Veiled Farm Girls is best if you use dried white bread that you have dried yourself. Then the sugared crumbs have a nut-like flavor as you crunch them through the soft applesauce and cream.

You may, of course, use packaged crumbs, but the result will not be the same.

4 servings

1 ¹/₂ lbs. apples	2 ¹/₂ tbsp. butter or
¹/₂ cup water	margarine
approx. ³/₈ cup sugar	
	1 ¹/₂–2 cups heavy
2 cups dried, ground	cream
white bread	(¹/₂ tsp. vanilla)
³/₈ cup sugar	

Peel the apples, cut them in wedges and remove core. Cook apples soft in the water. Be sure they don't scorch on the bottom of the pan. Sugar to taste. Stir to the consistency of applesauce, but leave a few whole bits of apple. Cool.

Melt the butter or margarine in a frying pan. Add the bread crumbs and sugar. Mix and brown over medium heat. Turn constantly with a spatula as they brown. The bread can easily burn if it is not stirred all the time. The sugared crumbs should have the color of light caramel. When done, pour onto a flat platter and cool.

Whip cream stiff, adding a little vanilla, if desired.

Layer bread crumbs, applesauce and whipped cream in a glass bowl. Place a layer of cream on top. Sprinkle with a few crumbs to garnish.

CLOUDBERRY CREAM
Moltekrem

The very name calls forth memories of golden-yellow cloudberry marshes that look untouched, even when your bucket is picked full; of aching backs that have bent time and again to gather a mouthful of the peerless berries; of roomy bowls, filled to the brim with the world's best Christmas dessert.

4 servings
2 cups heavy cream
1–1 ¹/₂ cups sugared
   cloudberries

Whip the cream stiff. Sugar the cloudberries to taste or use cloudberry jam. Mix berries with the cream. Serve with wreath cake (page 74) or other almond flavored cakes.

Or serve Cloudberry Cream in Krumkaker (page 94).

Veiled farm girls
Tilslørte bondepiker

POOR KNIGHTS
Arme riddere

Stale white bread can hardly be used to better advantage than in this dessert.

The bread slices are soaked in a mixture of egg and milk until they are wet through but not so soft that they don't hold together.

Poor Knights is a perfect dessert after a light dinner.

4 servings

8 thick slices of day-old white bread	1 1/4 cups milk
2 eggs	1/2 tsp. cinnamon
2 tbsp. sugar	butter or margarine for frying

Place bread slices in one layer on a platter or in a roasting pan. Beat the eggs with the sugar, milk and cinnamon and pour the mixture over the bread. Let stand for 20–30 minutes until thoroughly soaked. Turn the bread two or three times.

Fry the bread slices golden brown on both sides in the butter or margarine.

Serve poor knights warm with jam or red sauce (page 58).

RICH KNIGHTS
Rike riddere

These «knights» are both rich and potent. They are best served after a light meal, for example, a salad, a soup or a vegetable dish.

You may also serve rich knights as «cake» with after dinner coffee.

4 servings

4 slices of day old white bread	1 3/4 cups milk
2 tbsp. butter or margarine	4 tbsp. sugar
	1 tsp. cinnamon
3 large eggs	1/2 cup almond flakes

Slice the bread 1 inch thick. Brown on both sides in butter or margarine in a frying pan.

Place the bread in a pyrex mold or on an oven proof platter. Beat the eggs with the milk and half of the sugar. Pour it over the bread. Let stand 15 minutes so most of the liquid is absorbed. Sprinkle with cinnamon and the rest of the sugar and sprinkle almond flakes on top.

Bake the «knights» on the middle rack of the oven at 375 °F. (200 °C) for 15–20 minutes.

Be sure not to burn the almonds.

Serve rich knights warm, spread with jam and with a dollop of whipped cream or vanilla ice cream on top.

RICE CAKES
Rislapper

When we were children, if there was a little left-over rice porridge from Saturday's mid-day meal, we often had Rice Cakes for supper or with Sunday's after-dinner coffee.

When you make the batter for Rice Cakes, be sure to fry the cakes at once. If the batter stands it will get thin and not form cakes. Always fry a sample cake. Add a little more flour if the batter is too runny.

2 cups rice porridge (page 110)	2–3 eggs
2–3 tbsp. sugar	(1/4 tsp. vanilla)
1–1 1/2 cups flour	butter or margarine for frying

Mix the rice porridge with sugar, flour and the lightly beaten eggs. Amounts will depend on how thick the porridge is. Add a little vanilla, if you like.

Brown a little butter or margarine in a frying pan. Ladle spoonfuls of batter into the pan and smooth the surface so the cakes are equally large.

Fry the cakes golden brown on both sides.

Serve rice cakes right from the frying pan, spread with jam. Delicious with after-dinner coffee or for dessert.

Poor knights – Arme riddere
Rich knights – Rike riddere

BLUEBERRY PANCAKES
Blåbærpannekaker

In this recipe the blueberries are stirred into the pancake batter. You should fry a sample pancake to see if there is enough flour in the batter. The pancakes are best with as little flour as possible, but the batter must be thick enough for the pancakes to hang together.

The berries will burst when the pancakes are fried and the juice will run out into the frying pan. Rub the pan clean with paper towels after each pancake is done so the juice doesn't burn.

4–6 servings

3 eggs	1 quart blueberries
1 ¼ cups sour cream	a dash of salt
1 ¼ cups milk	1 tbsp. sugar
½–¾ cup flour	margarine for frying

Beat the eggs, first alone, then with the sour cream and milk. Sift in the flour. Beat well, until the batter is smooth. Add salt, sugar and blueberries.

Fry a sample pancake. Add more flour if the batter is too runny. Brown a little margarine in the frying pan and add a spoonful of batter. The cakes should be thick. Use low to medium heat so the cakes are cooked through without becoming too brown.

Fry all the pancakes and stack them on a warm platter.

Sprinkle with a little sugar and serve warm.

FRUIT SOUP
Fruktsuppe

Fruit soup, also called sweet soup, was formerly a popular everyday dessert. Any fresh or frozen berries, rhubarb, apples or dried fruit, together with fruit juice, may be used in this dessert.

4 servings

1 lb. apples, cut in wedges or 1 lb. rhubarb, diced	or 2–3 cups berries 1 quart water 2–3 tbsp. sugar
or ½ lb. dried fruit (prunes, apricots, mixed fruits)	1 ½–2 tbsp. potato flour or cornstarch

Dried fruit should be rinsed and allowed to soak in cold water for a couple of hours. Boil the fruit until it is soft. Then follow the instructions below to make the soup.

Boil fresh fruit or berries in the water with sugar and cook until soft. Add more sugar to taste.

Make a thickening of potato flour or cornstarch and a little cold water. Stir it into the soup and bring it to a full boil.

Serve the soup lukewarm or cold.

RICE CREAM
Riskrem

A flavorful fruit sauce should be served with Rice Cream. You may also make a sauce from the juice in a can of cherries, adding the cherries to the sauce.

4 servings

1 ½ cups heavy cream	2 ½ cups cold rice porridge (see page 110)
1 tbsp. sugar	
½ tsp. vanilla	25 scalded almonds

Whip cream stiff with the sugar and vanilla. Stir the rice porridge. Stir the almonds and porridge into the cream. Sugar to taste. Pour into a glass bowl. Garnish with a few chopped almonds.

NORWEGIAN PANCAKES WITH BLUEBERRY JAM
Pannekaker med blåbærsyltetøy

A traditional dessert, served after a pea soup supper, often a Saturday night meal. Pancakes with blueberry jam are a delicious dessert and taste good with a cup of coffee after dinner. Fresh sugared blueberries are even better than jam. It makes sense to freeze sugared blueberries in the fall, or freeze the berries without sugar and add the sugar when you thaw them.

4–6 servings

2 cups flour	margarine or butter for
1/2 tsp. salt	frying
2–3 tbsp. sugar	
3–4 cups milk	1 lb. blueberries
3 eggs	1/2 cup sugar

Mix flour, salt and sugar in a dry mixing bowl. Pour in half of the milk and stir to a smooth batter. Add the rest of the milk and the lightly beaten eggs. Let the batter stand and swell for about 1/2 hour. Fry thin pancakes.

Stack the pancakes with a strip of waxed paper between each, so it will be easier to separate them before serving.

Stir the blueberries and sugar to jam consistency.

Place the pancakes on a platter with a layer of blueberries on each pancake. Slice in wedges as a cake. Or fold the pancakes in triangles and serve the blueberries in a bowl on the side.

MOLDED RICE PUDDING WITH LINGONBERRIES
Risrand med rørte tyttebær

You must try this dessert! Many call it their favorite and almost everyone likes it. Lingonberries taste a little like cranberries, but are far more versatile. In the fall, laden with buckets and a picnic lunch, Norwegians flock to the woods to pick quart after quart of wild lingonberries.

The rice may be cooked and poured into the mold a day ahead.

Fresh lingonberries should be stirred with sugar until the sugar is dissolved.

Frozen lingonberries should be partly thawed before stirring or they will «take off» from the mixing bowl.

Rice pudding with lingonberries is good enough for a party dessert.

If you can not get lingonberries try raspberries or any other tart berry for this dessert.

4 servings
1 cup long grain rice
2 cups water

Boil the rice 20 minutes in the water. Pour the cooked rice into a colander and rinse it well with cold water. Drain very well.

Rinse a ring mold or a bowl with cold water or grease it well. Place the rice in the mold and press it firmly into the mold with the back of a spoon. Refrigerate until the dessert is to be served.

Turn the molded rice out on a platter. Fill the ring with freshly stirred lingonberries or, if you used a bowl as mold, surround the rice with the berries.

Rice and stirred lingonberries may also be served in separate bowls, each guest helping himself. Serve with cream.

Stirred lingonberries
1 lb. lingonberries
1/2 lb. sugar

Clean and rinse the berries. Stir them with the sugar until the mixture is light and fluffy and the sugar is dissolved. A rotary or electric mixer may be used.

The amount of sugar depends on how tart the berries are.

Stirred lingonberries are best freshly stirred. They are also well suited to freezing and taste as good as fresh when thawed.

Lingonberries may also be frozen unsugared in plastic bags. Stir sugar into the partly thawed berries, as needed.

CAKES
For coffee time

ALMOND WREATH CAKE
Kransekake

Wreath cake can be temperamental. Even if we make it in «exactly the same way» each time we bake it, the results may vary from absolute perfection to complete failure.

There are many different recipes for wreath cake. In some recipes the almonds are scalded, in others not. Some add a little flour to the dough, some knead the ingredients cold, while still others heat the dough in a saucepan. The recipe below takes a little extra time, but the cake is nearly always chewy and moist, just as it should be.

1 lb. almonds	**For mixing the next**
1 lb. powdered sugar	**day**
⅝ cup unbeaten egg	⅜ cup stiffly beaten egg
whites	whites

For the molds
melted butter or
    margarine
semolina or farina

Scald the almonds. Let them dry for 4–5 days.

Grind the almonds once in a nut grinder. Mix them with the powdered sugar and the unbeaten egg whites in a large saucepan. Knead the dough well with your hands. Place the pan over low heat and warm the dough, kneading constantly, until it is so hot that you burn your knuckles. Make sure the dough does not scorch on the bottom of the pan.

Set the pan aside on the kitchen counter. Cover tightly and let stand until the next day.

Next day: Add the 2 stiffly beaten egg whites to the dough and let it rest for 2 hours.

Brush the rings with melted butter while you wait, and let them stand 15–20 minutes until the fat hardens. Brush once more and strew semolina or cornmeal over the greased rings to ease removal of wreathes.

Press the dough through a pastry bag, or roll long ropes by hand. The ropes should be finger thick. If they are too thin they will be dry when baked. Place the ropes of dough in the cake rings and press the ends neatly together.

Place the rings on a cookie sheet. You will need several sheets.

Bake them for 12–15 minutes at 350 °F. (180 °C) on the middle rack of the oven. Continue baking on the bottom rack for about 5 minutes or until they are pale golden brown.

Cool the wreathes in the molds. Unmold the wreathes when they are cold and carefully brush off the semolina or cornmeal with a pastry brush.

Place the wreathes in a tightly covered cake tin. So that they will retain their moist chewiness, stretch a damp cloth tightly over the top of the tin, under the cover the night before the serving. Don't let the cloth touch the wreathes or they will be soft. Or place half a raw potato or a crust of soft bread in the container with the cake. Store the wreathes until they are to be used.

Or freeze them and thaw them in their container.

The wreathes are traditionally decorated with a powdered sugar icing as the cake is «built».

Icing
Mix ½ cup powdered sugar with a little egg white. Stir to a thick. smooth icing. Stir in very small amounts of egg white at a time. The icing should hold its shape and not be runny.

Pipe the tops and sides of the wreathes in even scallops.

Stack the wreathes with the largest on the bottom, forming a pyramid. Decorate with marzipan roses, bonbons, party snappers and small flags.

CREAM LAYER CAKE WITH FRUIT OR BERRIES
Bløtkake med frukt eller bær

A beautifully decorated, large, luscious cream layer cake always gives added spice to a special occasion. This recipe makes a big cake filled with lots of fruit or berries.

The cream is spread between the layers and is also used to decorate the cake. If you want to pipe cream around the edges of the cake you must allow twice as much cream as is called for.

4 eggs	1 cup flour
³/₄ cup sugar	1 tsp. baking powder

Beat the eggs and sugar until the sugar is dissolved and the mixture holds its shape – about 10 minutes. Sift in the flour and baking powder and fold in quickly and lightly. A rubber scraper is useful for this task.

Pour the batter into a well-greased 9 inch round cake spring mold.

Pre-heat the oven to 375 °F. (190 °C). Put in the cake and turn the thermostat down to 325 °F. (160 °C).

Bake the cake on the lowest rack of the oven at 325 °F. (160 °C) for 30–35 minutes. Test with a cake tester to see if the cake is done. The cake is done when no batter sticks to the cake tester and when it begins to loosen from the sides of the cake pan.

Let the cake rest a few minutes in the pan before carefully turning it out on a cake rack.

Filling

1–1 ½ quarts berries, for example, strawberries, raspberries, wild strawberries, cloudberries or sugared currants

or

3 bananas, mashed
³/₄ cup orange juice
1 sliced banana
½ lb. grapes, cut in two and seeded

or

1 can fruit cocktail
1 can mandarin oranges

1 jar apricot puré

or

1 package frozen strawberries
1 can of pears

or

1 can of pineapple, cut in pieces
1 can of peaches, cut in pieces

Decoration

1 ½–2 cups heavy cream
1 tsp. sugar
or 1 tsp. vanilla

Slice the cake horizontally into three layers. Place the bottom layer on a platter and the two others on waxed paper on the kitchen counter. Drip the layers carefully with a little milk mixed with ½ tsp. sugar, lemon soda, sweet white wine mixed with water, apple juice or other fruit juice. Never use strongly colored juices for this purpose. The cake is driest at the edges, so dampen it more there. But take care that the layers don't get too wet. Dip a pastry brush in the liquid, lay the flat side of the brush against the cake and «paint» it. In this way you have better control over the distribution of the liquid.

Drain the canned fruits if you are using them as filling and garnish. Fruits used for garnish should drain on paper towels.

Berries used for filling should be lightly sugared before they are spread between the layers. If you are using jam it should be spread on the cake before the cream.

Decorate the top of the cake with some of the same fruit or berries that it is filled with.

Whip the cream stiff.

Spread the layers with fruit and whipped cream and put them together. Spread the top and sides of the cake with cream and garnish with berries or fruit.

WHITE LADY
Hvit dame

Ask a man from Bergen what he considers the best cake in the world and he is sure to answer, «White Lady». This cake is a Bergen speciality and «the lady» is always present when Bergenites have a party.

The cake	Filling
3 eggs	¾ cup strawberry jam
½ cup sugar	2 ½ cups heavy cream
¾ cup flour	
¼ tsp. baking powder	**Cover**
	marzipan
Macaroon	walnut halves
¾ cup sugar	powdered sugar
½ cup hazelnuts	
1 ½ tbsp. flour	
2 egg whites	

Beat the eggs and sugar stiff in a double boiler. Sift the flour and baking powder together and fold them carefully into the eggs with a rubber scraper.

Pour batter into a greased 8 inch round cake tin with removable rim. Bake on middle rack of 350 °F. (175 °C) oven for about 30 minutes.

Cool the cake a few minutes before turning it out on a rack.

Wash, dry and grease the cake tin.

Grind the nuts for the macaroon in a nut grinder or in a blender. Mix the ground nuts with the flour and ½ cup of the sugar.

Whip the egg whites stiff with the rest of the sugar. Fold the nut mixture into the egg whites. This must be done carefully so the air that was beaten into the eggs is not stirred out again. It is this air that makes the macaroon rise.

Spread the nut mixture in the bottom of the cake tin. Bake on the middle rack of an 200 °F. (100 °C) oven for about 1 hour. The macaroon should be crisp and dry. Cool it on a rack. Whip the cream stiff.

Slice the sponge cake in three horizontally. One layer should be a little thicker than the other two. Place the thickest layer on a cake platter and spread with strawberry jam. Place the macaroon on top and spread with jam.

Spread with whipped cream and place a sponge cake layer on top. Spread with jam and cream and place the last cake layer on top. Cover the top and sides of the cake with whipped cream. Reserve a little, if you like, to decorate.

Roll the marzipan cover over the cake. Trim. Decorate with whipped cream rosettes and walnut halves. Sift a little powdered sugar over the top.

APPLE CAKE FROM JØLSTER
Eplekake fra Jølster

A delicious dessert cake that should be served in the pan.

2 lbs. apples	Cake batter
4 oz. raisins	¼ cup butter or
½ tsp. cinnamon	margarine
grated peel of 1 lemon	⅜ cup sugar
2 tbsp. sugar	3 eggs
2 tbsp. water	¾ cup ground almonds
	1 tbsp. flour

Core and peel the apples. Slice them. Place apple slices, raisins, grated lemon peel, cinnamon, sugar and water in a wide-topped saucepan. If the apples are tart, add a little more sugar. Cook covered until the apples are soft. Shake the pan now and then. Cool.

Stir butter or margarine light with half of the sugar. Separate the eggs. Add the egg yolks, flour and ground almonds to the butter and sugar.

Beat the egg whites with the rest of the sugar and fold them carefully into the batter.

Grease an oven proof dish or a cake tin, about 9″ in diameter. Put half of the batter in the dish and bake on the middle rack of the oven at 350 °F. (180 °C) for 10–15 minutes, until golden.

Lay the cooled apple slices, raisins and nuts on the baked cake bottom and cover with the rest of the batter. It will not cover the fruit, but spread it out as well as possible. The surface will expand during baking.

Bake the cake for a further 15–20 minutes.

Serve lukewarm with cream.

White lady – Hvit dame

MANOR HOUSE APPLE PIE
Herregårdseplekake

There are so many apples in the filling for this deep dish pie that it is truly moist and delicious. If the apples are very tart you can sprinkle them with more sugar.

The almond topping is temptingly crisp with the flavor of pralines. Be sure the topping does not get too browned. To avoid this you can slide a cookie sheet onto the top rack of the oven to lower the heat. Or cover the cake with waxed paper.

Pastry	Filling
$3/4$ cup butter or margarine	2 lbs. apples
$1 1/4$ cups flour	$3/8$ cup sugar
$1/4$ tsp. salt	$3/4$ cup raisins
$1/2$ cup sugar	1 oz. almonds
1 egg	
2 tbsp. cream	**Almond topping**
	$2 1/2$ oz. butter or margarine
	$3/8$ cup sugar
	1 oz. almonds

Make the pastry first: Mix flour, salt and sugar and crumble the butter or margarine into the mixture. Make a hollow in the flour and pour in the egg and cream. Knead the dough quickly together. Wrap it in plastic and refrigerate at least an hour.

The dough may also be made in a food processor: Place flour, salt and sugar in the bowl with the cold butter, diced. Run the steel blade until the mixture has the consistency of coarse crumbs. Add the egg and cream and run the blade until the dough forms a ball. Stop the machine at once. Take out the dough, press it together, wrap in plastic and refrigerate. The pastry may be made a day ahead.

Roll the dough out $1/8$ inch thick. Dust counter top with flour so the pastry doesn't stick to the surface.

Butter a 9 inch round cake tin with removable rim. Cut out two pastry circles to fit the tin. Place one in the bottom of the tin and reserve the other for the top. Press the leftover pastry around the sides of the tin so that all the dough is used.

Peel the apples. Cut them in quarters and core. Thinly slice the apple wedges. Place them in the pastry shell and sprinkle each layer with sugar, raisins and scalded, chopped almonds. Place the second pastry circle on top and press the dough tightly to the sides of the pastry walls.

Prick the pastry cover with a cake tester or a fork.

Mix butter or margarine, sugar and the finely chopped almonds to a light and porous mass. Spread the mixture on the pastry cover. Place the pie on a piece of aluminum foil on a cookie sheet and fold the foil up along the edges of the tin. Fat is apt to leak from the tin during baking. Bake the pie on the lowest rack in the oven at 350 °F. (180 °C) for about 1 hour. Serve the pie luke warm or cold with stiffly whipped cream.

Manor house apple pie
Herregårdseplekake

KVÆFJORD CAKE OR «THE WORLD'S BEST»
Kvæfjordkake eller «Verdens beste»

You may wonder at the small amount of batter in this recipe. The dough is spread thinly over the pan. You will be pleasantly surprised when the cake is done and you see how much the cake and meringue have risen.

$^1/_2$ cup butter or margarine	$^3/_4$ cup flour
$^1/_2$ cup sugar	1 $^1/_2$ tsp. baking powder
4 egg yolks	1 tsp. vanilla
	4 tbsp. milk

Grease a rectangular cake tin, about 8 × 15 inches. Line it with waxed paper. Let the paper extend a ways out of the pan for the cake rises a good deal. Grease the paper lightly.

Cream butter or margarine and sugar until light. Add the egg yolks and vanilla. Mix baking powder with flour and add alternately with the milk.

Spread the batter evenly over the bottom of the pan.

Meringue

4 egg whites	$^1/_2$ cup coarsely chopped almonds
$^7/_8$ cup sugar	

Beat the egg whites stiff. Beat in the sugar a little at a time until it forms a stiff mass. Spread over the top of the cake batter and sprinkle with coarsely chopped almonds.

Bake the cake on the middle rack of the oven at 350 °F. (175 °C) for about 25 minutes.

Cool the cake a little in the tin and slide it with the paper onto a wire rack. The cake should not be inverted.

Filling

Make vanilla cream from a mix or from scratch. Add a about 1 $^1/_2$ tsp. gelatin. Fold in a little whipped cream.

Slice the cake in two horizontally. Spread cream on the bottom half and place the other on top.

Whipped cream may also be served in a bowl on the side with the cake.

PRINCE CAKE
Fyrstekake

«Fyrstekake» is one of the «greats». This recipe calls for plenty of almond filling, making it especially delicious.

Prince cake should «rest» for a day before it is eaten.

The cake keeps well and may be frozen.

	Almond filling
$^3/_4$ cup butter or margarine	10 oz. almonds, about 2 cups
$^5/_8$ cup sugar	2 cups powdered sugar
2 egg yolks	$^1/_4$ tsp. vanilla
2 tbsp. cream	$^1/_2$ tsp. baking powder
1 $^3/_4$ cups flour	5 egg whites
2 tsp. baking powder	

Stir sugar or margarine and sugar until light and porous. Add the egg yolks and cream. Add flour and baking powder, sifted together.

Grease a 9–10 inch round cake tin with a removable rim. Press $^3/_4$ of the dough onto the bottom of the cake tin and about 1 inch up the sides.

Add a little more flour to the rest of the dough, wrap it in plastic and refrigerate.

Grind the unscalded almonds for the filling. Beat egg whites stiff. Fold in the almonds, the sifted powdered sugar, the vanilla and the baking powder. Spread the filling evenly over the dough in the tin.

Roll out the rest of the dough. Cut it into narrow, even strips, preferable with a pastry wheel. Lay the strips crisscross on top of the cake. Lay strips of dough around the edges.

Brush the dough strips with egg white or egg yolks beaten with a little water.

Bake the cake on the lowest rack of the oven at 350 °F. (175 °C) for 45–50 minutes.

Let the cake stand for a few minutes before removing the rim. Let it stand 15–20 minutes more before carefully removing it from the bottom of the cake tin and placing it on a wire rack.

BERLIN BUNS – JELLY DOUGHNUTS
Berlinerboller

Berlin buns are best fresh and warm.

14–15 buns

2–2 ½ cups flour	thick raspberry jam,
2 tsp. sugar	apricot puré or
¼ tsp. salt	vanilla cream
⅜ cup margarine	
½ cup milk	**For deep frying**
2 oz. yeast	1 lb. lard
2 eggs	

Mix flour, sugar and salt and crumble in the margarine. Heat the milk to lukewarm. Stir the yeast into the milk. Make a hollow in the middle of the flour. Add the yeast and the lightly beaten eggs.

Mix the dough lightly. It should be thoroughly mixed but do not over-mix or the dough will be tough. Let stand covered 5–10 minutes. Turn out on counter top and roll it out to ¼ inch thick sheet. Sprinkle plenty of flour under the dough so it doesn't stick to the counter.

Mark rounds lightly on half of the dough with a glass. Spoon ½ tsp. of the filling you choose in the middle of the round. If there is too much filling it is apt to leak out of the buns when they are cooked. Lay the other half of the dough loosely over. Cut through both layers of dough, making sure that the jam comes in the middle of each round. Use a glass or cup with a dull rim so the two layers are pressed together. If the glass is too sharp the layers will separate during cooking.

Press the two layers firmly together along the edges with your fingers.

Press the leftover dough together. (It should not be kneaded as it will become tough.) Roll out and proceed as above. Continue in this fashion until all the dough is used. If too much loose flour sticks to the buns, brush it off with a pastry brush. Cover the buns with a cloth and let rise in a warm place for about 20 minutes. If the buns rise too long they can swell and deflate.

Heat the fat for deep frying in plenty of time, so it may heat slowly and safely. The fat is hot enough when it bubbles around the handle of a wooden spoon.

Fry a sample bun. Use a slotted spoon to place them in the fat. The buns should be round and plump. Turn them often. Do not let the cooking element get too hot. Don't fry more than 2–3 buns at once. They should be evenly browned and cooked through. Remove the buns from the fat and drain them on paper towels. Roll them in sugar or sprinkle with a little powdered sugar.

SVELER

If you have ever taken the ferry in Romsdalen in Western Norway you may well have tasted «Sveler» in the cafeteria on board. Sveler are traditional in Northern Møre County and are often served with after-dinner coffee. Sveler have a low fat content, yet they are filling. They are inexpensive and easy to make.

2 eggs	approx. 2 ¼ cups flour
½ cup sugar	1 tsp. baking soda
1 ½ cups buttermilk or	a dash of salt
yoghurt (If yoghurt	
is used the sveler	
will have a slightly	
acidic flavor.)	

Beat eggs and sugar together thoroughly. Add the buttermilk and sift in the flour, mixed with the baking soda and salt. Beat the batter smooth and lumpfree. Let the batter stand and swell for 20–30 minutes.

Grease a frying pan. Use a bit of waxed paper to hold the margarine or shortening for easier greasing. Allow a large spoonful of batter for each cake. Smooth the surface of the batter in the pan with the spoon.

Fry «Sveler» light brown on both sides. Do not use too high heat as then the cakes will brown without cooking through. Butter the cakes when they are cold and sprinkle with sugar, or try them with Norwegian brown goat cheese, «geitost».

COFFEE CAKE WREATH
Kringle

This luscious almond filled yeasted wreath is usually served at Norwegian birthday parties.

2 oz. yeast	**Almond filling**
1 ³/₄ cups milk	*1 cup almonds*
¹/₂ cup butter or	*³/₈ cup butter or*
* margarine*	* margarine*
¹/₄ tsp. salt	*¹/₂ cup sugar*
¹/₄ cup sugar	*2 egg yolks*
1 tsp. cardamom	
¹/₂ egg	
4–4 ¹/₂ cups flour	

Melt the butter or margarine. Add the milk and heat to lukewarm. Dissolve the yeast in a little of the milk. Add the rest of the milk. Add salt, sugar, half of the flour with the cardamom, and half of a lightly beaten egg. Knead in more flour, a little at a time, until the dough is smooth and pliant but not tough. Let rise in a warm place until double in bulk.

Grind the almonds, scalded or not, as you prefer.

Mix the butter and sugar together and add the almonds and egg yolks.

Turn the dough out on the counter. Divide it in three parts, two large and one smaller. The smallest part is used as the «backbone» of the wreath, the two larger ones are the rounded sides and lengths that cross each other.

Roll the two largest pieces of dough into ropes about 18 inches long. Pat them flat and roll with a rolling pin until they are about 6–7 inches wide.

Roll the smallest piece of dough to a 9 inch long rope. Roll it with the rolling pin until it is about 6–7 inches wide. Spread the almond filling onto each length of dough, leaving a thin strip of dough uncovered on each side. Brush the uncovered edges with egg and fold them over the almond filling, pressing lightly so they stick. Place them with the seam down on a cookie sheet covered with waxed paper. Form a wreath with the shorter piece at the back and the two longer pieces on each side. Let rise well for about 30 minutes. Brush the top and sides of the wreath carefully with the rest of the beaten egg. Sprinkle with a little coarse sugar and slivered almonds.

Bake on the lowest rack of the oven at 375 °F. (200 °C) for 20–30 minutes.

SUCCESS TART
Suksessterte

This cake is well named. A cake filled with so many good things can not fail to be a success.

4 egg whites	*1 heaping cup*
1 cup powdered sugar	* unscalded almonds*

Beat the egg whites stiff. Add the sifted powdered sugar and beat a little longer.

Chop the almonds fine in a blender or grind them in a nut grinder. Fold the ground almonds carefully into the stiffly beaten egg whites.

Line a cookie sheet with waxed paper. Draw two circles about 10 inches in diameter on the paper. Brush the paper with melted margarine. Spread the dough evenly on the circles.

Bake the cakes on the middle rack of the oven at 300–350 °F. (160–170 °C) for about 15 minutes.

Turn the cakes out onto a wire rack. Pull the paper off while the cakes are warm. Cool them.

Butter cream

4 egg yolks	*1 cup powdered sugar*
³/₄ cup heavy cream	*¹/₂ cup butter*

Mix egg yolks, cream and the sifted powdered sugar in a small saucepan. Place over low heat and stir until the mixture thickens. Cool.

Stir butter soft. Add the egg mixture, a spoonful at a time.

Spread half of the butter cream onto one of the cakes. Place the other cake on top and spread with the rest of the cream.

Garnish with grated bittersweet chocolate.

Success tart
Suksessterte

WAFFLES WITH FRESHLY STIRRED JAM
Vafler med nyrørt syltetøy

Waffles are served as dessert or with after-dinner coffee in Norway, not for breakfast.

10–12 waffles

1/4 cup butter or margarine	2 eggs
2 1/2 cups flour	1/2 cup heavy cream
3 cups milk	1/4 tsp. salt
	2–3 tbsp. sugar

Melt and cool the butter or margarine.

Put flour in a mixing bowl. Make a hollow in the middle and pour in half of the milk. Stir to a smooth batter. Add the lightly beaten eggs, cream, melted butter or margarine, salt and sugar.

Let the batter stand and swell for 20–30 minutes.

Heat the waffle iron. Grease it for the first waffle. Pour the batter on the iron in small ladlefulls and fry golden brown on both sides.

Stirred raspberry jam
1 pint of raspberries
about 1/2 cup sugar

Stir berries and sugar together until the sugar is dissolved.

SUNDAY WAFFLES
Søndagsvafler

If you want a special treat with Sunday coffee, try these waffles. Right from the waffle iron, spread with good jam they are «heavenly».

3 cups flour	4 eggs
4 tbsp. sugar	1/2 cup melted butter or margarine
2 tsp. baking powder	
3 cups milk	

Mix flour, sugar and baking powder in a bowl. Make a hollow in the dry ingredients and pour 2/3 of the milk in. Beat the batter smooth. Add the rest of the milk.

Add the egg yolks to the batter with the melted, cooled butter or margarine.

Beat egg whites stiff and fold them into the batter. Grease the waffle iron with melted margarine for the first waffle. Fry the waffles golden brown. Cool on a rack.

BUNS
Hveteboller

Light as a feather buns are as popular with children as with adults. Serve them whole or split in two with butter and jam or brown goat cheese.

24 buns

	Glaze
1/2 cup margarine	
1 3/4 cups milk	1 egg
2 oz. yeast	2 tbsp. water
1/2 cup sugar	
1 tsp. cardamom	
approx. 3 1/2 cups flour	

Melt the margarine, add the milk and heat to body temperature. Dissolve the yeast in a little of the milk and add the rest. Add sugar and most of the flour with the cardamom. Knead the dough smooth and pliant. Use as much flour as is needed.

Cover the bowl with a cloth and let rise for about 30 minutes.

Turn the dough out on the counter and divide it into 24–30 pieces, according to how large you want the buns. Roll them into smooth balls with the palm of your hand and place them a bit apart on a cookie sheet that has been greased or covered with waxed paper.

Cover the buns with a cloth and let rise in a warm place until they are well risen.

Brush lightly with egg beaten with water.

Bake on the lowest rack in the oven at 425 °F. (225 °C) for 10–12 minutes. Cool on a rack.

Waffles – Vafler

STRIBOLTs

BOK- OG PAPIRHUS

2600 LILLEHAMMER

Forf.: Horvig, Ingrid Espelid

Tittel: The best Norwegian traditional Cuisine

Bok nr.:

Forl.: Jyld 05-20-57-79

Utk.: 1997

Pris: Kr 198,-

Hylle: 32

Dato	Ant.
6/8 92	3
2./0	1
9. /2	7

Vennligst returner dette kort til oss
hvis de ved en feil har fått det.

a-Trykk a.s. Lillehammer

CHRISTMAS CAKES AND COOKIES

ROSETTES

For this recipe you need a special rosette iron.

³/₄ cups flour	**For deep frying**
³/₄ cup skimmed milk	*1 lb. lard or fat for deep*
2 eggs	*frying*
2 tbsp. sugar	
¹/₄ tsp. salt	

Mix flour and milk to a smooth batter. Add salt and sugar. *Stir* in eggs. Do not beat the batter or there will be air bubbles in it. Let the batter stand and swell for about 30 minutes.

Heat the fat as for hartshorns (see page 92). Dip the rosette iron into the fat and heat it well. Shake off the fat and dip the iron into the batter just to the top of the iron. If you dip it deeper the cakes will not loosen from the iron. Dip the iron into the fat. Do not get it too near the bottom of the kettle. Loosen the rosette from the iron when it starts to turn color. Turn the rosettes carefully. They should be golden brown on both sides. Remove them from the fat and turn them out on absorbent paper to drain.

BERLIN WREATHES
Berlinerkranser

Berlin wreathes are very brittle and should be removed from the baking sheet with care. Cool on a wire rack.

1 hard boiled egg yolk	**Glaze**
1 raw egg yolk	*1 egg white*
4 tbsp. sugar	*coarse sugar*
about 1 ¹/₄ cups flour	
¹/₄ lb. butter or	
margarine	

Hard boil an egg. Remove the yolk and mash it thoroughly. Add it to the raw egg yolk. Add sugar and stir stiff with a wooden spoon or in an electric mixer. Crumble the butter or margarine into the batter alternately with ³/₄ of the flour. Add the egg mixture. If the batter is very soft you may add a little more flour. Save the rest for rolling out the cakes.

Knead the dough lightly until it is thoroughly mixed, but no more. Too much kneading can make the dough dry and difficult to roll. This is also the case if you add too much flour.

Break off small pieces of dough. Roll them into ropes, pencil thick. Cut them into 5 inch lengths. To ensure equal lengths, cut a strip of cardboard 5 inches long and use it as a measure for cutting the ropes of dough.

Shape the ropes in rings, pressing them together, letting a little bit of each end stick out. The protruding ends should not be too long or they will break off.

The cookies will be easier to handle if they are chilled well before glazing.

Brush the wreathes with slightly beaten egg white and dip them in coarse sugar. Hold the wreathes where the ends cross. Place the wreathes on a greased cookie sheet. Bake them on the middle rack in the oven at 350 °F. (180 °C) for about 10–12 minutes, until they are golden.

Hart's horn – Hjortetakk
Poor man – Fattigmann
Berlin wreathes – Berlinerkranser

DOUGHNUTS
Smultringer

If you are working alone, it is a good idea to cut out a number of doughnuts before you begin to fry them. Pile leftover dough together and pat or roll it out. The dough must not be worked too much or it will be tough and difficult to roll. The doughnuts will then be dry and not as good.

2 eggs	*1 level tsp. baking*
³/₄ cup sugar	*powder*
³/₄ cup heavy cream	*approx. 3 cups flour*
³/₄ cup low fat sour	
cream or buttermilk	**For deep fat frying**
¹/₂ tsp. cardamom	*about 1 lb. lard*

Beat the eggs and sugar together until stiff. Whip the cream and add cream and sour cream or buttermilk to the eggs.

Mix flour, cardamom and baking powder, and sift into the egg mixture. Knead the dough until all the ingredients are well mixed.

The dough should not be tough. Refrigerate a while.

Roll out a little of the dough at a time into ¹/₂ inch thick sheets.

Cut with a doughnut cutter.

Heat the fat in a fryer or kettle until a cube of white bread turns golden brown in 1 minute or until the fat boils around the handle of a wooden spoon.

Place 3–4 doughnuts in the fat at once. Turn them when they float to the surface. Fry them golden brown on both sides.

Thread the doughnuts onto the handle of a wooden spoon and drain them. Place them on a wire rack covered with absorbent paper.

Cool the doughnuts before storing them in a cake box or in the freezer.

VANILLA RINGS
Vaniljekranser

Vanilla rings were traditional Christmas cakes in grandmother's day.

1 ¹/₂ cups butter or	*1 ¹/₄ cups sugar*
margarine	*2–3 tbsp. cold water*
3 ¹/₂ cups flour	*1 tsp. vanilla*
1 tsp. baking powder	

Mix flour and baking powder. Crumble in butter or margarine. Add sugar and water and knead the dough quickly.

Press dough through a pastry tube with a star pattern attachment in long ropes on a cutting board. Cut the ropes in 5 inch equal lengths. Cut the ends at a slight angle so it is easier to piece them together and the seams will be less visible. Place the rings on a cookie sheet, greased or covered with waxed paper. Bake 10–12 minutes at 350–375 °F. (180–200 °C).

SAND TARTS
Sandkaker

Special sand tart tins are used for these cookies, but it is possible to use standard muffin tins. Do not grease the molds.

¹/₂ lb. butter or	*¹/₂ cup ground*
margarin	*almonds, scalded or*
1 ¹/₂ cups powdered	*not*
sugar	*2 ³/₄ cups flour*
1 egg	

Beat butter or margarine and the powdered sugar white.

Add egg, ground almonds and flour. Refrigerate dough overnight. Press a ball of dough the size of a walnut, into sand tart molds or standard muffin tins. Bake golden brown on the middle rack in the oven at 350 °F. (180 °C) for about 15 minutes.

Invert the molds on a platter. As they cool, the tarts will fall out of the molds. Press the bottom of the mold *lightly* if the tarts stick.

Store sand tarts dry and cool in a tight cake tin. Or freeze them. The tarts will thaw on the serving platter and taste just as good as if freshly baked.

POOR MAN
Fattigmann

Poor men should be pale and tempting, thin and crisp. They should be stored in a cake box with a tight lid.

8 egg yolks	$^1/_2$ tsp. cardamom
8 tbsp. powdered sugar	2 $^1/_2$ cups flour
8 tbsp. heavy cream	
1 tbsp. cognac	**For deep frying**
	1 lb. lard

Beat the egg yolks and 6 tbsp. of the powdered sugar stiff. Whip the cream stiff with 2 tbsp. of the powdered sugar. Stir together eggs and cream. Add the cognac and cardamom. Fold in about 2 cups of the flour. The rest of the flour is used on the counter top for rolling out the dough.

Cover the dough and refrigerate overnight.

Turn the dough out on the counter top and roll it with your hands to a long, thin sausage. Do not knead too much or it will be tough. Cut off a small portion at a time and roll to a thin sheet, leaving the rest of the dough in the refrigerator. With a pastry wheel, cut strips 2 $^1/_2$ inches wide. Cut the strips at an angle in 4 inch lengths with the pastry wheel. Poor men may also be made larger, if you wish. With the wheel, cut a small slit in the middle of each cookie and thread one point of the dough through the hole. Place the cookies on a cutting board to transport them to the stove.

Heat the lard or other fat in a deep fat fryer or in a deep, heavy bottomed kettle. The fat is hot enough when a cube of white bread turns golden brown in 1 minute or when the fat boils around the handle of a wooden spoon.

Do not place more than three poor men in the fat at a time. It is hard to watch more. Turn the cookies as soon as they float to the surface or there will be bubbles in the dough. Turn the cookies a couple of more times. They should be pale golden yellow. Remove them with a fork when they are done. Shake off a little of the fat and place them on a wire rack over absorbent paper so the paper catches the fat.

SERINA COOKIES
Serinakaker

These cookies belong to the familiar, favorite cookies served at Christmastime.

$^5/_8$ cup butter or margarine	$^1/_2$ tsp. vanilla
$^5/_8$ cup sugar	$^1/_4$ tsp. baking powder
1 egg	egg to glaze
1 $^1/_2$ cups flour	$^3/_4$ cup coarsely chopped almonds

Beat butter or margarine and sugar light. Add vanilla. Add egg and beat well. Sift in flour and baking powder and mix the dough lightly. Refrigerate for 2–3 hours until it is stiff.

Roll out small balls of dough. Press the balls a little flat with a fork. Brush with lightly beaten egg and sprinkle with coarsely chopped almonds.

Bake Serina cookies golden brown at 350 °F. (180 °C).

OATMEAL MACAROONS
Havremakroner

Store the oatmeal macaroons in a tightly covered cake tin.

1 cup minus 1 tbsp. butter or margarine	1 tsp. cinnamon
1 $^1/_4$ cups sugar	$^1/_2$ tsp. clove
$^1/_2$ cup milk	1 $^1/_2$–2 tsp. baking powder
1 $^3/_4$ cups flour	2 $^1/_2$ cups whole oats

Stir butter or margarine and sugar light. Mix flour, spices and baking powder and add alternately with milk. Add whole oats. Drop the batter from a teaspoon on a greased cookie sheet. Bake the cookies pale golden brown at 350 °F. (180 °C). Cool on wire rack. Store in a tightly covered cake tin. Or freeze them in suitable containers.

HART'S HORN
Hjortetakk

The three incisions in the outside of each ring suggest the horns of the hart.

³/₈ cup butter or margarine	¹/₂ cup heavy cream
4 eggs	1 tsp. grated lemon zest
1 cup sugar	¹/₂ tsp. cardamom
	approx. 3 ¹/₂ cups flour

1 tsp. hartshorn salt, ammonium carbonate (If hartshorn salt is not to be had, use baking powder which will give a slightly different consistency to the cookies.)

For deep frying
1–2 lbs. lard

Melt and cool the butter or margarine. Beat the eggs and sugar stiff. Whip the cream. Mix the eggs, cream, melted fat and grated lemon zest. Add flour mixed with the cardamom and hartshorn salt.

Mix the dough well but do not over mix.

Cover with plastic and refrigerate overnight.

Roll the dough into pencilthick ropes. Cut it into 5 inch lengths. Cut at a slight angle so the ends can be neatly pieced together into rings.

Cut three incisions in the outside of each ring or leave them uncut, if you prefer.

Place the cakes on a lightly floured surface. Roll out all the cakes before starting to fry.

Heat the lard in a deep kettle. It is hot enough when a cube of white bread turns golden brown in about 1 minute or when the fat boils around the handle of a wooden spoon.

Fry a sample cake.

Do not place more than 5–6 cakes in the fat at once. The cakes should come to the surface quickly. Turn them – preferably with a wooden dowel, the handle of a wooden spoon, or the like. Do not fry them too brown. Thread the cakes onto the dowel or spoon handle and let them drain over the kettle.

Place them on a wire rack covered with absorbent paper.

GORO

Goro are made with a special iron. There are many handsome old goro irons. Should you be fortunate enough to own one, try it for fun. Modern goro irons are made from cast iron. They are efficient and have an attractive pattern.

Making goro is time-consuming. It is best to have help with the work so that one person can roll out the dough while the other fries the cookies.

You may use just butter or just margarine in goro dough, or mix in a little of the lard that is left over from deep frying.

Fat will leak out of the iron while you are cooking the goro. Wipe it regularly off the stove with paper towels so it doesn't smoke.

3 small eggs	or part butter and part lard
1 ¹/₄ cups sugar	
1 lb. butter or margarine	¹/₄ cup cold water
	4 ³/₄ cups flour
	1 tsp. vanilla

Melt butter, margarine or butter and lard. Cool. Beat egg and sugar stiff. Add water. Add vanilla. Stir in flour alternately with fat. Mix the dough well but do not over mix. Cover dough with plastic and refrigerate overnight.

Cut a cardboard the same size as the goro iron.

Roll small bits of dough to thin sheets. Cut them, using the cardboard pattern. Place the sheets of dough on a lightly floured surface. If you are working alone it is wise to cut out all the sheets before you start to cook them. Place waxed paper between the sheets of dough, stack several on top of each other and refrigerate them until you are ready to cook them. They will be easier to handle.

Heat the iron on the stove top. Use a burner that is the same size as, or larger than, the iron. Place the sheets of dough in the iron and press the top down so the pattern on the iron is clearly reproduced on the cookies. Cook goro pale golden brown on both sides. Remove them from the iron with a pancake turner. Place the cookies on a cutting board and cut them apart.

GENUINE HONEY CAKE
Ekte honningkake

This honey cake also belongs to the Christmas season. It is moist and delicious and keeps well if it is stored in an air-tight container in a cool place. Honey cake may also be frozen.

	Flavoring
³/₄ cup butter or margarine	¹/₄ tsp. ground clove
7 oz. honey	2 tsp. ginger
³/₈ cup sugar	¹/₂ cup chopped candied orange peel
3 eggs	
1 ³/₄ cups flour	about ¹/₂ cup raisins
1 tsp. baking powder	

Mix butter or margarine, honey and sugar until light. Add eggs, one at a time, and stir well. Add the flavorings.

Sift flour and baking powder together and add. Pour the batter into a greased 1 ¹/₂ quart loaf pan. Bake on the lowest rack in the oven at 350 °F. (175 °C) for 50–60 minutes. Place a cookie sheet on the top rack of the oven if the loaf browns too fast.

STRULL

This is another cookie that requires a special iron.

Strull should be wrapped around a pencil or thin dowel. The cookies are fine accompaniments to whipped cream desserts, such as Bavarians, but are also good, just as they are, with after- dinner coffee.

1 ¹/₄ cups thick sour cream	³/₈ cup sugar
	⁷/₈ cup flour

Beat the sour cream with the sugar. Add the flour and let the batter stand and swell for about 30 minutes.

Heat the iron. Place a big spoonful of batter on the iron and smooth the surface. Press the top of the iron down on the batter, but not too hard or the batter will run out. Cook strull pale golden-brown on both sides. Lay them on a cutting board and roll them at once around a pencil or wooden dowel.

CHRISTMAS LOAVES FROM BERGEN
Bergensk julekake

These popular loaves are served in many Norwegian homes during the Christmas holidays.

¹/₂ lb. margarine, or	⁷/₈ cup sugar
	approx. 6–7 cups flour
6 oz. margarine and 2 oz. butter	1 ¹/₂ tsp. cardamom
	1 tsp. salt
2 ¹/₂ cups milk	8 oz. raisins
3 oz. yeast	3 oz. candied fruit peel

Melt the margarine or margarine and butter. Add the milk and heat lukewarm. Dissolve the yeast in a little of the liquid. Mix milk, yeast, sugar and about half of the flour, mixed with cardamom and salt. Knead the dough well. Cover the mixing bowl with a cloth and let dough rise for about 30 minutes.

Turn dough out on counter top and knead in raisins, candied peel and the rest of the flour. The dough should be firm. Cover it again and let rise 30–40 minutes more.

Divide the dough in two. Make round balls. Place them on a cookie sheet covered with waxed paper. Make incisions around the loaves with a sharp knife and press the dough balls with your fist in the middle of the top. Cover the loaves with plastic and a cloth and let rise about 1 hour. Beat an egg with 1 tbsp. water and brush the loaves twice with the mixture to glaze.

Place the cookie sheet on the bottom rack in the oven and bake them for 5 minutes at 425 °F. (225 °C). Turn the thermostat down to 375 °F. (200 °C) and bake them 35–40 minutes more.

To avoid over-browning place a cookie sheet on the top rack of the oven to lower the temperature.

Cool the loaves on a wire rack.

CURLED COOKIES OR CONES
Krumkaker

These cakes require a special «krumkake» iron.

You can also make «bowls» of curled cookies. Lay the warm cookies over the bottom of a glass. Turn a cup carefully over the cookie to make neat bowl shapes. These are delicious filled with berries and whipped cream or with ice cream for dessert.

3 eggs	*5 oz. butter or*
³/₄ cup sugar	*margarine, melted*
1 cup flour	*¹/₄ tsp. vanilla, optional*
	¹/₄–¹/₂ cup water

Beat eggs and sugar stiff. Add flour and vanilla, if desired. Melt and cool the butter or margarine. Add to batter. Let batter stand and swell about 30 minutes. Add a little cold water if the batter is too thick.

Heat the «krumkake» iron. Place a big spoonful of batter on the hot iron. Press the top down well so the cookies are thin and crisp. Turn the iron quite soon so the cookies are evenly cooked on each side. Test the heat. It is best to cook curled cookies slowly so they do not get too brown.

Place a cutting board by the stove. Place the cookies on the board while they are warm and roll them around a wooden «krumkake» cone. The cakes stiffen quickly, so work fast. Put more batter on the iron as each cone is shaped.

SYRUP SNIPS
Sirupssnipper

Syrup snips are diamondshaped cookies that belong to the favorite cookies made for Christmastime.

¹/₄ cup sugar	*¹/₄ tsp. ginger*
3 oz. dark cane syrup	*¹/₂ tsp. pepper*
¹/₄ cup table cream	*¹/₂ tsp. baking soda*
¹/₄ cup margarine	*1 ¹/₂–1 ³/₄ cups flour*
1 egg yolk or ¹/₂ egg	*scalded almonds*

Bring syrup, sugar and cream to a boil. Pour them over the margarine and stir until melted. Add egg yolk or the ¹/₂ egg, lightly beaten, and cool mixture to lukewarm. Sift a little of the flour with the spices and baking soda. Add to the batter. Sift in more flour until the dough is firm and can be kneaded. Don't add more flour than necessary to hold the dough together. Cover dough and refrigerate overnight.

Roll out the dough in convenient amounts in thin sheets. Don't use too much flour for this. Loose flour on the cookies makes them gray. Cut diamonds, about 2 × 4 inches, with a pastry wheel. Place half a scalded almond with the flat side down, in the middle of each diamond before baking.

Place the cookies on a cookie sheet that has been greased or covered with waxed paper. Bake at 350 °F. (180 °C) for 8–10 minutes, until nicely browned. When the cookies are done, cool them on a wire rack.

COOKIE MEN
Kakemenn

Children love to bake and it is a real treat for them to help make and decorate theese cookie men.

¹/₂ cup margarine	*baking powder*
1 ³/₄ cups sugar	*1 ¹/₄ cups milk*
1 tsp. hartshorn salt or	*approx. 6 cups flour*

Melt and cool margarine. Mix the dry ingredients. Add the melted margarine and stir quickly to a smooth dough. Cover with plastic and refrigerate 1–2 hours. Knead the dough lightly and roll out to a thickness of about ¹/₈ inch. Cut figures with cookie cutters. Place on a greased cookie sheet and bake at 375 °F. (200 °C) for 7–10 minutes. The figures should be white and porous when they are done.

Cool cookies on a wire rack. Mix vegetable coloring with a little water and brush eyes, nose, mouth and some streaks indicating clothes on the cookie men.

MOTHER MONSEN
Mor Monsen

No one knows who Mother Monsen was, but her cake is a favorite at Christmas.

	Garnish
1 cup plus 1 tbsp. butter or margarine	½ cup scalded almonds, cut in fine strips
1 ¼ cups sugar	
6 eggs	
grated zest of 1 lemon	½ cup dried currants
1 ¾ cups flour	3–4 tbsp. granulated
1 tsp. baking powder	sugar

Stir butter or margarine and sugar until creamy.

Add eggs, one at a time, and stir thoroughly after each addition. Add the grated lemon zest. Mix flour and baking powder, and add.

Pour the batter into a 8 × 16 inch pan, lined with waxed paper and well greased. Smooth the batter out evenly in the pan. Sprinkle with granulated sugar, currants and almonds. Press the garnish *lightly* into the batter so it doesn't fall off when the cake is done.

Bake on middle rack of the oven at 375 °F. (190 °C) for 20–25 minutes. The cake should be pale golden-brown and baked through, but not dry! Remove it from the oven as soon as no batter sticks to an inserted cake tester. Let stand a few minutes in the pan.

Place a piece of waxed paper over the cake. Lay a cookie sheet on top and turn the cake pan upside down on the sheet. The cake will then rest bottom up on the cookie sheet. Place a wire rack on the upturned cake and turn again so the cake rests right side up on the rack. Cool the cake on the wire rack.

When the cake is cold, cut it in diamonds with a very sharp knife.

SYRUP CAKE
Sirupskake

This cake is quickly made and tastes particularly good accompanied by a cup of coffee or tea.

5 cups flour	3 cups buttermilk, if preferred or use yoghurt which will give a slightly more acidic flavor
½ tsp. pepper	
1 tsp. ginger	
2 tsp. baking soda	
1 cup sugar	
	1 cup cane syrup
	1 pkg. candied peel

Sift flour, spices, baking soda and sugar together. Make a hollow in the middle and add most of the milk. Stir quickly together. Warm the syrup so that it flows freely and mix it into the batter. The syrup should not be hot, but just lukewarm, so that it is easier to mix. Add the candied peel. The mixture should have the consistency of a thick loaf cake batter. Regulate by adding milk if it is too thick.

Grease an oblong cake pan, about 7 × 11 inches. If you line the bottom with waxed paper, it will be easier to turn out the cake. Pour in the batter. Bake cake on the bottom rack of the oven at 325 °F. (170 °C) for ¾–1 hour. Keep an eye on the cake so it doesn't get too brown. Cover with waxed paper if necessary. Test the cake with a cake tester. It should come out clean.

Cool the cake briefly in the pan before turning out on a wire rack. The surface of the cake has a tendency to stick to the rack so it is a good idea to place waxed paper on the rack before inverting the cake. Cut the cake in two or three, lengthwise, when it is cold. Slice to serve.

This cake keeps well in a covered tin in a cool, dry storage room.

Mother Monsen
Mor Monsen

CHRISTMAS STOLLEN
Julekake i form

Christmas stollen is served with other kinds of bread at Christmas. It is delicious buttered, topped with brown goat cheese (geitost), and accompanied by a cup of coffee or tea.

This recipe will fill two 2 quart or three 1 ½ quart loaf pans.

about 6–7 cups flour	*3 cups milk*
1 ½ cups margarine	*2 eggs*
1 ⅛ cups sugar	*2 oz. yeast*
1 tsp. cardamom	*7 oz. raisins*

Crumble the margarine into the flour. Add sugar and spices. Heat the milk lukewarm. Stir the egg and yeast into the milk. The yeast should be completely dissolved. Knead the milk and flour mixture to a firm, pliant dough. Cover dough with plastic and a cloth. Let rise to double in bulk. Turn the dough onto the counter top. Divide it into two or three equal pieces. Divide the raisins among the pieces and knead them into the dough. Make loaves and place them in greased loaf pans. The pans should only be half full. Cover with a cloth. Let rise for about 30 minutes. Brush with lightly beaten egg or with an egg yolk mixed with a little water.

Bake the loaves on the lowest rack of the oven at 350 °F. (175 °C) for about 50 minutes.

Cool the loaves on a wire rack.

PEPPER NUTS
Peppernøtter

These cookies are quite sweet and a little hard, but have excellent flavor.

2 small eggs	*½ tsp. ginger*
1 ¼ cups sugar	*½ tsp. ground black*
8 oz. cane syrup	*pepper*
½ cup melted butter or	*½ tsp. star anise*
margarine	*½ tsp. baking powder*
½ tsp. cinnamon	*approx. 3 ½ cups flour*

Beat egg and sugar stiff. Add syrup and the melted, cooled butter or margarine. Sift in 3 cups of the flour, the spices and the hartshorn salt. Mix to a smooth dough. Save the rest of the flour for making the cookies.

Cover dough with plastic wrap. Refrigerate overnight. Roll the dough to long ropes, cut them in equal lengths and make balls.

Bake on the middle rack of the oven at 350 °F. (180 °C) until golden brown.

MALT LOAF FROM BERGEN
Bergensk julevørterbrød

This is a dark loaf with a wonderful spicy flavor. It is only baked at Christmas and is served buttered with brown goat cheese, head cheese or lamb roll.

Two large loaves	*approx. 4 ½ cups*
2 ½ cups water	*white flour*
2 oz. yeast	*1 tsp. salt*
6 oz. dark cane syrup	*1 tsp. ground clove*
⅜ cup sugar	*2 tsp. star anise*
2 ½ cups rye flour	*10 oz. raisins*

Heat water to lukewarm. Stir in yeast. Add syrup, sugar, rye flour and half of the white flour, spices and salt. Knead to a smooth dough. (With an electric mixer, if you like.)

Cover the mixing bowl with a cloth. Let rise about 1 hour. Knead in the raisins and more of the flour. The dough should be firm, but it may not be possible to knead in all of the flour. Knead well. The better the dough is kneaded, the better the result.

Let rise again for about 1 hour, covered with plastic and a cloth.

Turn out on counter top and divide in two. Shape long loaves. Place them on a cookie sheet covered with waxed paper. Let rise about an hour. Brush once with lightly beaten egg. Bake the loaves at 375 °F. (200 °C) for about 40–45 minutes.

Malt loaves brown fast. If your oven has top heat, lower it to 350 °F. (180 °C), or place a cookie sheet on the top rack of the oven, or cover loaves with foil.

TEMPTING BREAD

RYE BREAD
Grovt rugbrød

A little vinegar in bread dough makes it firmer and gives the bread a slightly acid flavor that goes well with caraway seed. Caraway is a traditional bread seasoning. Bread made with rye flour stays moist longer than bred made only with wheat.

2 large loaves

1 ¼ cups bran	1 tbsp. vinegar, 5 %
1 ¼ cups lukewarm water	3 tbsp. vegetable oil
	3 tbsp. dark syrup
3 oz. yeast	1 ½ tsp. caraway seed
3 cups lukewarm buttermilk or sour milk	(may be omitted)
	3 ½ cups rye flour
	approx. 3 ½ cups
2 ½ tsp. salt	white flour

Place the bran in the mixing bowl and add water. Mix well. Crumble the yeast in the water. Add milk, salt, vinegar, oil, syrup and caraway, if used. Stir in rye and white flour and mix well. Knead the dough until it is firm and pliable. Brush a little oil on top. Cover with a cloth and let rise for about 45 minutes in a warm place.

Turn the dough out on a floured surface. Divide in two and shape two loaves. Put them in two greased 1 ½ quart loaf pans. Cover and let rise about 30 minutes.

Bake loaves on lowest rack in oven at 375 °F. (200 °C) for about 1 hour.

WHOLE RYE BREAD
Grovt brød

This is a good every day bread. Be careful not to let the dough get too firm. Regulate the texture of the dough with white flour. Bread dough should be soft to the touch and easy to shape. Thorough kneading is important for a smooth, pliant dough. Kneading also gives the bread a firmer crumb, making it better to slice.

2 loaves

2 tbsp. margarine or 3 tbsp. vegetable oil	½ cup wheat bran
	1 cup whole rye flour, coarsely ground
3 ¼ cups water	approx. 5 ½ cups
2 oz. yeast	white flour
1–2 tsp. salt	

Melt margarine, add water and heat mixture to lukewarm. Or add oil to the warm water.

Dissolve yeast in a little of the liquid. Mix all ingredients together, reserving a little of the white flour. Knead, adding a little flour at a time, until the dough is firm and pliant.

Cover dough bowl with plastic and a kitchen towel.

Let rise 30–40 minutes.

Turn dough out on a floured surface. Divide in two. Knead each piece well, using a little more flour, if necessary. Shape two loaves.

Place the loaves in two well greased 1 ½ quart loaf pans. Cover with kitchen towel and let rise again for 30 minutes.

Bake bread on lowest rack in oven and bake at 375 °F. (200 °C) for about 1 hour.

Cool on rack.

WHOLE WHEAT BREAD
Helkornbrød

Salt gives bread extra flavor and makes it keep better. Bread may be baked without salt, but then the amount of yeast should be increased to make it rise better.

3 loaves

10 oz. wheat kernels	4 cups coarsely milled
2 cups water	whole wheat or
4 cups water or	graham flour
skimmed milk	approx. 7–8 cups
2 oz. yeast	white flour
1 tbsp. salt	

Place the wheat kernels to soak in 2 cups of water for 3–4 hours or overnight.

Heat 4 cups of water or skimmed milk lukewarm. Dissolve yeast in a little of the liquid and add to rest of liquid. Stir in salt, whole wheat or graham flour and white flour to make a firm, pliant dough. Add the soaked wheat kernels.

Cover bowl with a cloth and let rise in a warm spot until double in bulk.

Turn dough out on floured surface. Divide in three and knead each part well, using more flour as required. Shape three loaves and place them in greased 1 ½ quart loaf pans. Cover loaves with a cloth and let rise for about 30 minutes.

Brush loaves lightly with lukewarm water.

Bake on lowest rack in oven at 375 °F. (200 °C) for about 1 hour.

If you use ordinary aluminum loaf pans it is a good idea to take the loaves out of the pans when they are nearly done. Bake them for the last 15 minutes on a cookie sheet. This gives the loaves a crisp brown crust on all sides. If you use non-stick bread pans it is not necessary to remove the loaves as an even, crisp crust is formed in the pans.

SOUR DOUGH RYE BREAD
«Surbrød»

This bread is somewhat like dark Danish rye bread. It is moist and flavorful and goes particularly well with salt herring and with brown Norwegian goat cheese, «geitost».

3 large loaves

2 cups cold water	2 ½ cups coarsely
1 cup wheat kernels	ground whole rye
	flour
	½ oz. yeast

Mix all ingredients, cover with a kitchen towel and let stand in a warm place for 12–20 hours to sour the dough.

Add:

1 ½ quarts lukewarm	2 ¾ cups coarsely
water	milled whole rye
2 oz. yeast	flour
2 tsp. salt	2 ¾ cups finely milled
2 tsp. caramel coloring	rye flour
1 cup wheat bran	
1 ¾ cups white bread	
flour	

Mix and knead the dough thoroughly. Cover with plastic and a kitchen towel and let rise about 30 minutes.

Divide dough into three equal parts. Shape loaves and place them in greased 1 ½ quart loaf pans. The dough will be a bit sticky, making it difficult to knead. Press the dough down in the pans so that the surface is even. Cover with a towel and let rise until the loaves fill the pans.

Brush the tops with a little water and sprinkle with rolled oats, if you like.

Bake on bottom rack in oven at 375 °F. (200 °C) for about 1 hour. Cool on rack. Wrap loaves in plastic or aluminum foil. Let them mature a day before eating. Cut thin slices with a sharp knife.

This bread may be frozen.

OAT BREAD
Havregrynsbrød

Rolled oats give bread extra flavor and a moist consistency. This bread is a little sweet, a trait that many people appreciate.

Syrup also helps make the loaf keep well.

2 loaves

4 cups skimmed milk	*2 ³/₄ cups finely milled*
2 oz. yeast	*whole wheat flour*
3 tbsp. vegetable oil	*approx. 2 ³/₄ cups*
2 tbsp. dark cane syrup	*white flour*
1 ¹/₂ tsp. salt	*rolled oats for topping*
2 ³/₄ cups rolled oats	

Heat milk lukewarm. Crumble yeast in a mixing bowl. Stir in a little of the milk to dissolve yeast. Add the rest of the milk.

Add vegetable oil, syrup and salt and stir in rolled oats, whole wheat flour and most of the white flour. Knead in flour until the dough is firm and pliant but not tough.

Knead well. Or beat about 5 minutes at half speed with an electric mixer.

Cover bowl with plastic and a cloth and let rise about 40 minutes. Turn it out on a floured surface. Divide in two. Knead in a little more flour and shape two loaves. Place in well-greased 1 ¹/₂ quart loaf pans.

Let rise again under a cloth for about 30 minutes.

Brush with a little lukewarm water and sprinkle with rolled oats.

Bake on lowest rack in oven at 375 °F. (200 °C) for about 1 hour.

Cool loaves on rack.

Oat bread should stand overnight before it is sliced.

SIFTED BREAD
Siktebrød

This bread used to be very popular in Bergen. The name refers to the fact that the bread was baked of only finely sifted flour. Rye flour makes the crumb a bit grayer than bread baked of only wheat flour.

2 loaves

4 cups skimmed milk	4 cups finely milled rye flour
1 oz. yeast	about 4 cups white bread flour
2 tsp. salt	

Heat milk to lukewarm. Crumble yeast in mixing bowl and dissolve it in a little of the milk. Add the rest of the milk. Stir in salt and flour. Regulate consistency of dough with white flour. Knead thoroughly until firm.

Cover dough with a kitchen towel and let rise in a warm place about 1 hour.

Turn out on floured surface. Knead in more flour, both white and rye, until the dough is firm and pliant.

Divide dough in two and shape loaves.

Place loaves in greased 1 ½ quart loaf pans or on an 8 × 12 inch oblong cake pan. If you use the latter, place the loaves toward the sides of the pan so there is an opening between them. Remember to grease the sides of the loaves that face each other with melted margarine.

Cover with a cloth and let rise to double in bulk. They should fill the pan.

Brush with warm water and prick the surface with a fork.

Bake on bottom rack in oven at 375 °F. (200 °C) for about 50 minutes.

Cool on a rack.

«HALF FINE» RYE BREAD
«Halvfint» brød

This is also an old Bergen stand-by. It is even grayer than sifted bread, but it has a moist crumb and a delicious, slightly sweet flavor.

2 loaves

4 cups skimmed milk	3 ½ cups coarse rye flour
1 oz. yeast	approx. 3 ½ cups white bread flour
2 tbs. dark syrup	
2 tsp. salt	
1 ¾ cups fine rye flour	

Heat milk to lukewarm. Crumble yeast in mixing bowl and dissolve in a little of the milk. Add the rest of the milk. Add syrup, salt and flour. Knead until the dough is firm and pliant.

Cover with plastic and a cloth and let rise in a warm place for about 1 ½ hours.

Turn dough out on a floured surface. Knead in more coarse rye flour if necessary, until the dough is easy to handle.

Divide in two and shape loaves. Place them in greased loaf pans or in an 8 × 12 inch oblong cake pan. Remember to grease the inside of the loaves if you use an oblong pan.

Cover with a kitchen towel and let rise for 15–20 minutes.

Brush with warm water and prick surface with a fork.

Bake on lowest rack in oven at 375 °F. (200 °C) for about 50 minutes. Test to see if loaves are done by knocking on the bottom or, if the loaves are baked in a cake pan, by pressing lightly against the inner sides. The bread should spring out after light pressure is applied.

Cool on rack.

LUMPER OR POTATO CAKES
Lumper eller potetkaker

In many parts of Norway lumper are called potato cakes. Potato cakes have traditionally been served as «cakes» with after dinner coffee. They are spread with butter and geitost or sugar, with sour cream and jam on special occasions. Lumper or potato cakes are also served for breakfast or supper with other sandwich spreads.

In our day lumper are commonly used to wrap around hot dogs.

Mash or rice the potatoes while they are warm. If you want to use leftover potatoes, heat them in a little boiling water for a few minutes. Pour off the water and dry the potatoes in the pan before you mash them.

Large amounts of potatoes may be ground in a meat grinder, preferably twice, with a little salt.

You can also make lumper with only 4–5 potatoes. Mash them fine and beat them firm with a fork or rub them through a sieve or ricer.

8 cups potatoes boiled in their peels	1 ¹/₂–2 cups flour, white, rye or barley
1 tsp. salt	

Peel the potatoes and grind them once or twice with the salt while they are still warm. Cool.

You may use only white flour or a mixture of white and rye, or white and barley.

It is important not to use too much flour in lumper. Stir in just a little at a time. If dough made from potatoes and flour is not used at once, but is left for a while, it will become moist and soft and be nearly impossible to bake.

Lumper may be made in several different ways:
With your hands, pat two small pieces of dough into small, round, not too thick cakes.

Or roll pieces of dough into round cakes with a rolling pin or a bottle.

Or roll out the dough in one large piece and cut it into suitable rounds with a pan cover.

Lumper should be about ¹/₈ inch thick and about 6 inches in diameter.

Brush off any loose flour before frying.

Fry lumper in an ungreased frying pan or on a griddle.

Use medium heat so the cakes don't get too brown before they are cooked through.

If the heat is too high the cakes may stick to the pan and burn on the surface while they are still raw inside.

If bubbles form while the lumper are frying, prick them with a fork.

Stack the cakes and wrap them in a kitchen towel as they are finished. The stored heat will keep them soft.

Lumper are best right from the griddle, but they may be cooled, wrapped in plastic and refrigerated for a couple of days.

If lumper stand at room temperature too long they will mold.

Lumper freeze well.

FLAT BREAD
Flatbrød

There are innumerable flat bread recipes, but this dough is easy to roll out and bake. It is a good recipe for the beginner.

Much the same equipment is used for flat bread as for lefse. A standard flat bread griddle is 18 inches in diameter. If you are using a smaller surface you should make more sheets of flat bread. A grooved rolling pin is best to use for rolling out the dough. These are to be had in all Norwegian shops that sell kitchen equipment.

12–15 pieces

3 cups barley flour	¹/₄ tsp. salt
1 ¹/₂ cups coarsely ground whole wheat flour	1 tbsp. sugar
	2 ¹/₂ cups milk
1 ¹/₂ cups rye flour	1–1 ¹/₂ cups water

Mix flour, salt and sugar. Heat milk and water to body temperature. Add liquid to flour a little at a time and stir to a firm dough.

Divide in 12–15 parts and roll out in paper thin round sheets 13–15 inches in diameter with a grooved rolling pin. Turn the dough a few times and lift from the counter top so it is aired, thus keeping the dough from sticking. Flour the work surface with barley flour. When the dough is large enough for your griddle, brush away all loose flour. Place the sheet of dough on the griddle and fry at medium heat until it is crisp and cooked through. Turn and fry briefly on the other side.

Store flat bread in a dry place.

SHINY LEFSER
Blanke lefser

A «lefse» is a kind of pancake. It is eaten buttered and spread with sugar, jam or geitost.

16 lefser

3 $\frac{1}{2}$ cups milk	3 $\frac{1}{2}$ cups white bread flour
$\frac{1}{2}$ cup semolina	
$\frac{3}{8}$ cup heavy cream	**Glaze**
$\frac{1}{2}$ cup margarine	3 eggs
$\frac{1}{2}$ cup sugar	$\frac{3}{4}$ cup milk

Bring milk to a boil. Stir in semolina and add cream, margarine and sugar. Simmer about 10 minutes to the consistency of thick porridge. Put flour in a mixing bowl. Pour in the boiling porridge and stir to a firm dough.

Scrape dough out of bowl on to a floured surface and shape to a sausage. The dough will be so soft that it can not be rolled. Divide into 16 pieces. Place them in a large plastic bag so a crust doesn't form on the surface.

Heat a round electric flat bread griddle, if you have one, or use a large, ungreased griddle. It should be hot, but not so hot that the lefser burn. Rolling is easier if you do it on a pastry cloth or a piece of unbleached muslin.

Pat each piece of dough round and flat with flour before you roll it out. Flour the cloth, place the dough on it and roll to a large, thin, round sheet $\frac{1}{8}$ inch thick and 13–15 inches in diameter. Use a light touch on the rolling pin. The dough is soft and if you use a heavy hand you may make creases in the dough. Check constantly that there is still flour under the dough so it doesn't stick to the surface.

Roll the round sheet of dough over the rolling pin and unroll it on the griddle.

Fry it until it is dry on the under side. Turn and fry a couple of minutes on the other side. Beat egg and milk in a bowl. Brush the surface of the lefse with the egg mixture. Cook the lefse until there are no visible damp spots. Turn it and fry it briefly on the glazed side or until any damp, raw portions are cooked. Cool on a rack and stack the lefser when they are cool. Press under a light weight.

THIN LEFSE
Tynnlefse

This type of lefse is common in many parts of Norway.

12–13 lefser

5 cups white bread flour	3 cups milk
	1 oz. yeast
$\frac{1}{4}$ cup soft margarine	2 tbsp. water
2 tbsp. sugar	1 tsp. baking powder

Put flour, margarine and sugar in a bowl. Bring milk to a boil and pour it over the flour. Beat the milk into the flour with a wooden spoon. Stir as little as possible. The batter should not be tough.

Cool to lukewarm. Dissolve yeast in a little water and add it to the batter with the baking powder. Knead to a smooth dough.

Turn dough out on counter top and make a sausage. Cut into 12–13 equal parts. Place in a plastic bag or wrap in plastic so a crust doesn't form on the surface of the dough.

Press each piece of dough flat with the palm of your hand and roll to a thin round sheet $\frac{1}{8}$ inch thick and 13–15 inches in diameter. Flour the counter top so the dough doesn't stick. Heat the griddle. Fry the lefse until it is light colored and «dry» on top. Turn the lefse and fry it a little on the other side. The side that is cooked last will have many small brown spots. This is the «nice» side that should be visible when the lefse is buttered and folded. Place a light weight on the stack of lefser as they are finished.

All dry lefser should be soaked before they are buttered. Hold the under side of each lefse under running lukewarm water. Lay the first lefse right side up on a damp cloth. Stack the other lefser on top, with a damp cloth under each. Let them stand for 20–30 minutes until they are soft. Butter with softened butter and sprinkle with sugar and, if you like, cinnamon.

Fold two sides of the lefse toward the middle. Fold the edges in a little. Fold in half again in an even oblong, and cut in equal slices at a slight angle.

PORRIDGE
Our oldest warm dish

SOUR CREAM PORRIDGE
Rømmegrøt

In former times sour cream porridge was only eaten on special occasions. It was brought as a gift to the new mother during her lying in. It was served at weddings and funerals, to celebrate the harvest and to feed neighbors who gave a helping hand at busy times. The porridge was made from sour cream, flour and salt. The best sour cream porridge was so rich that it «danced» in the kettle in its own fat – food that was heavy and hard to digest. In our day we usually dilute the porridge with a little milk.

Sour cream porridge is most often made with white flour, but you may also use barley flour or a mixture of white flour and semolina. In some communities it is traditional to alternate layers of sour cream porridge with semolina pudding in the bowl, making a dish that is less rich and easier to digest.

Accompaniments to sour cream porridge are also strongly tied to tradition. Some people serve the porridge with salted herring or with poached fish, salted or fresh. Others serve cured salted ham, «spekeskinke» (prosciutto), salami and other salted meats with sour cream porridge.

It is popular to sprinkle the porridge with sugar and cinnamon. Fruit juice or milk is drunk with sour cream porridge.

4–5 servings

3 ½ cups thick sour cream	3 ½ cups milk
1 ½ cups flour	1 tsp. salt

Put sour cream in a kettle and stir until it boils. Leave the cover halfway off the kettle and simmer for 10 minutes.

Sift flour on a piece of waxed paper. Stir half of the flour into the sour cream. Simmer the porridge until the butter rises to the surface. Stir constantly so the porridge doesn't stick to the bottom of the pan. Simmer porridge until there is enough butter to skim off the porridge. Use a tablespoon or a small ladle to remove the fat and serve it with the porridge. Do not remove all of the fat or the porridge will lose its flavor.

Stir in the rest of the flour. Add milk, a little at a time, and bring the porridge to a boil after each addition.

Simmer for 8–10 minutes so the porridge will not taste of flour. Stir from the bottom now and then.

If sour cream porridge is to stand for a while before it is served, spoon a little milk on top to keep a skin from forming. Cover tightly.

Sour cream porridge gets thicker as it stands. It is a good idea to reserve a little milk to thin the porridge with before serving, if necessary. Bring the porridge to a boil before serving. Pour the melted butter over the porridge or serve it on the side.

Some people like raisins as well as cinnamon and sugar on their sour cream porridge.

Sour cream porridge
Rømmegrøt

VELVET PORRIDGE
Fløyelsgrøt

Velvet porridge bears its name with justice. It glides smoothly over the tongue and just plain makes you feel good. The satiny, glistening porridge even looks like velvet. It is not strange that children dream of big bowls of velvet porridge with lots of cinnamon and sugar on top...

Velvet porridge is made with butter and flour, in the same way as an ordinary white sauce. But make the porridge thicker.

4 servings

³/₄ cup butter or margarine	8–9 cups milk (a little salt)
1 ³/₄ cups flour	

Melt the butter or margarine in a heavy bottomed saucepan. Stir in the flour. Add the milk, a little at a time, and stir constantly so the porridge will be smooth and without any lumps. If you boil the milk before adding it, you will save a little time.

Simmer porridge for 8–10 minutes. Stir from the bottom now and then, so the porridge doesn't stick and burn. The porridge will thicken after it is cooked, so reserve a little milk to thin it. Many people think that the salt in the butter or margarine makes it unnecessary to add more salt, so taste the porridge before you adjust the seasoning.

Serve with cinnamon and sugar, and with glasses of milk or fruit juice to drink.

RICE PORRIDGE
Risengrynsgrøt

Rice porridge is just as popular today as it always was and it will surely continue to be a welcome treat on Saturdays, the traditional porridge day, or on any other day.

Its mild flavor and rich, granular consistency appeals to both children and adults.

This recipe calls for short grained, «porridge» rice. In the old days rice porridge was often after-cooked in a box lined with hay, newspapers or other insulating material. A pillow was placed on top as a cover.

The same effect may be attained by putting the tightly covered pan of boiling porridge in a cold oven. The oven walls act as insulator, and the porridge continues to cook «under its own steam».

Bring the porridge to a boil on the stove top before serving, and salt to taste.

4 servings

4 cups water	6–8 cups milk
1 ³/₄ cups short grained rice	approx. 1 ¹/₂ tsp. salt

Bring water to a boil, sprinkle rice in water and simmer covered for about 20 minutes until the water is absorbed.

Add milk and continue cooking on the stove top or in a cold oven. Use only 6 cups of milk if the porridge is to be cooked in the oven, as no liquid will be lost in steam. The porridge should boil, covered, for a couple of minutes before it is placed in the oven.

On the burner the porridge should cook for about 1 hour. Stir thoroughly now and then, so the porridge doesn't stick to the bottom of the pan and burn.

In the oven the porridge will need 2–3 hours. The door of the oven must not be opened during that time.

Season to taste with salt.

Serve rice porridge with sugar and cinnamon, and, if you like, with a dab of butter.